SWING TRADING METHOD USING OPTIONS

SWING TRADING METHOD USING OPTIONS

ON ETF

SUDIPTA DATTA

Arrow Books

Director of Marketing: Amy Moore
Executive Editor: Mary Wilson
Cover Designer: Kristy Harris

Published by Arrow Books
2967 Dundas St. W Suite 675
Toronto ON M6P 1Z2
Canada

Arrow Books
P.O. BOX 446
Houston TX 77411
USA

SWING TRADING METHOD USING OPTIONS ON ETF
ISBN-13 979-8-9884094-0-3

Library of Congress Cataloging-in-Publication Data
SWING TRADING METHOD USING OPTIONS by/Sudipta Datta
Library of Congress Control Number: 2023909605

Printed in the United States of America

To my late father-in-law Mr. P.C. Mukhopadhyay: with fond memories, love and deep respect

Contents

FOREWARD

The majority of the trading books that I have read preface with one of the following two categories in general: either a "rag to the riches" story (i.e. first and foremost, financial ruin and the subsequent epiphany and redemption) or "I, (the last "Market Avatar"), came, I traded, I conquered" type. (I must also admit that there are a considerable number of books about the subject, belonging to the *third* and more credible category such as John Carter's book, *Mastering the Trade* and Hill, Pruitt and Hill's book *The Ultimate Trading Guide* etc.).

I, however, have neither credentials under my belt. Neither did I borrow $700 from my brother-in-law to start trading and became rich; nor did I produce 259% returns in less than seven months with some *magical* (read "hocus, pocus") trading system and created a mob of ecstatic followers.

My story is straightforward and simple. I grew up in India and most of my youth were spent in a state where, the Communist regime (analogous to undivided Soviet Sovereign States) prevailed. Although, I had degrees in Engineering and Technology from a reputable Indian university and a good job in a renowned Multinational Company of Indian origin, I disliked the political system over there and wanted to get out.

So, in one snowy and lonely January 1996 evening, I landed in New York City with my spouse, my work visa, four suitcases and our diplomas in my attaché. Like most non-immigrants in temporary work visas, our initial days were a little rough; and although we were very conversant in English, we did not have a proper understanding of the *soul* of this country. After floating around for some years in different states of the United States, in 2001, we settled in Michigan where I was offered a senior position in a Blue Chip Company.

Meanwhile back home, my father retired from work and successfully invested his modest savings in National Savings Certificates (equivalent to T-Notes). During its heydays, those certificates offered non-taxable 12% per annum (or more) interest to double the money in six years (or less). It was one of the safest investments in India backed by the government with its never-cold money printing machines in the mints. Even these days, you can find Indian banks offering checking interest rates between 6-7% and for the savings accounts, you can expect even more.

However, in this country, I found a different story altogether. Here seven years T-Note offers merely 1.80% in treasury auctions; bank *boasts* of their highest in nation checking account yields as 1.79% and their formally-dressed executive takes *pride* to mention you that they also offer the highest yield savings account as high as 1.96%.

Such ridiculously *low* offerings of interest rates on so-called "safer" investments and the worrying thought of long-term shortfall (thus insolvency) of the Social Security developed a permanently unsettling feeling on me that, unlike my father, I could never retire. And adding insult to injury, I was also overwhelmed by the most expensive, just-downright-unreasonable and superfluous surcharges banks slap to their customers like the Minimum Balance / Monthly Maintenance Fees, Deposited Check Returned Fees, Early Account Closure / Inconvenience Fees, Teller Fees, Transaction Search / Investigation Fees, etc.

This apocalyptic disclosure of my subsequent doom helped me realize that I could never achieve financial freedom by investing upon those so-called safer investments and I alone need to take charge of my financial destiny. If I cannot manage my own money, no professional money manager can ever do it for me. Thus, I repelled Mutual Funds and managed futures as well.

And my trading journey began in parallel to my professional career. The trading started in a predicted sinusoidal path having both elating crests and humiliating troughs. During those crests, trading appeared deceptively easy to me and I took wild risks only to realize that it was sheer dilution. The market taught me big lessons during those troughs and I became sober and almost insolvent.

During that time, every well-wisher around me doubted my sanity and advised me to continue with my professional job only and to quit trading altogether as "95% of the retail traders lose money". Even my shoe shiner friend at Detroit airport suggested me to gamble instead and frequent Las Vegas; at least there the food is better. However, learning to trade became a never ending endeavor to me (I'm still learning in every moment of it) and I read, researched, analyzed and exposed my hard earned savings to risk again.

My trading subsequently made improvement when I realized that trading is nothing but a concoction: a recipe consisting of about 80% psychology, 15% financial risk management and merely 5% market technique.

I also realized that as 95% retail traders lose money, to be profitable in this game, we need to be contrarians and do the opposite of what retail traders do. These commoners are taught about the traditional market techniques and eventually get tricked by the "superpowers" (read National and International Money Center Banks, large Hedge

Funds etc.) exploiting the collective mentality of the herd. This realization was like a "nirvana" to me.

This book is nothing but a detailed roadmap of the off-beaten contrarian path to reaching the financial destiny with traversing techniques, alerts and warnings. **And I request every reader to go through the "Endnotes" in each chapter; they contain many "preliminary" information on the topic which were not contained in the main text and also sometimes very interesting other tit-bits.**

An old and famous Wall Street adage (by perhaps Bob Dinda of Merrill Lynch) was "There are old traders, there are bold traders, but there are no old, bold traders" *[Please see, The Wit and Wisdom of Wall Street by Bill Adler Homewood, IL: Dow Jones-Irwin 1985]*. This maxim simply means - a risky trading philosophy doesn't have much longevity. So, if you are an old (but not a bold) trader, I hope this book alters how you view your trading world and renews it with some smart, thought provoking and useful notions. If you're an aspiring trader, I'd also like to welcome you to this journey.

ACKNOWLEDGEMENTS

This book is a synthesis of ideas and concepts I've encountered in my readings, research, my profession in financial arena and various visceral and intellectual experiences. I have very few original ideas and virtually every diverse concept presented in this book has been congregated from somewhere else to produce a coherent whole.

In this adventure, firstly I'd like to thank my editor at Arrow Books, Mary Wilson, for her patience, efforts and excellent suggestions on making everything (magically) appear in a book form.

No book is ever complete without multiple drafts of the manuscript. In this token, I'd like to thank my learned friend Mr. Raja Ray for his editorial efforts, comments and suggestions in an earlier draft of this text.

I'm grateful to my two young adult sons Sabarno and Anwesh for their continuous encouragement, support and excitement. As a matter of fact, they were the ones who suggested that I should write this book; it was not in my "bucket" list. They also took personal interests in this project and I'm thankful for all their efforts.

My brilliant, beautiful and loving wife, Aparna, has always been immensely supportive of all of my endeavors, even though a majority of them were futile. I appreciate her tremendous persistence in this project. I would like to thank her for every great thing she's done for me, rain or shine.

I'd also like to thank our two "best" Fido boys, Honu (meaning green turtle in Polynesian language) and Mocha (meaning banana flower in my mother tongue), for keeping their strict eyes on dad's health by rarely allowing him to stay sedentary at his desk (to write this book) by insisting on non-stop playing.

Finally, the walk of life is a journey we cannot undertake alone. Along the road, countless women and men come to terms with who and what they are and love who and what they are; they make our journey of life simply fascinating: I bid my thanks to them all.

One

Introduction

ANY REASON TO BE IN THE MARKET IN THE FIRST PLACE?

> *"October. This is one of the peculiarly dangerous months to speculate in the market. The others are July, January, September, April, November, May, March, June, December, August and February."* - Mark Twain

Traders are speculators and most speculators are technical analysts. They speculate the market by using technical indicators and / or price action (like Japanese candlestick studies, tape reading etc.), which is a pure form of technical analysis.

Technical analysis holds that prices already reflect fundamentals (economic factors that influence the way the investors price financial markets) and so, fundamental analysis is no longer necessary and technical analysis alone will suffice.

This is essentially the First Dow Theorem [1] which states that "the market discounts everything". Thus, all of the fundamental factors like demand, supply and more are priced into the market, even before investors are aware of them. In stricter readings, even future events are discounted in the form of risk. On this point, Dow Theory agrees with one of the premises of the Efficient Market Hypothesis (discussed below).

Unfortunately, there is a wide rift between technical analysis and the academia. The proponent of "Random Walk Hypothesis" (RWH), economist Burton Malkiel *[2]*, compared the technical analysis to "astrology at best" in his book. To many scholars, day traders (they are 100% technical analysts) are "noise" traders. RWH claims that the market prices change at "random" and thus cannot be predicted. In theory, Random Walk Hypothesis is a derivative of the weak-form "Efficient Markets Hypothesis" (EMH). In a seminal paper in May 1970 issue of the Journal of Finance, economist Eugene Fama *[3]* proposed the EMH, which contradicts the basic tenets of technical analysis by stating that past prices cannot be used to profitably predict future prices. Thus, it holds that technical analysis cannot be effective as current prices reflect all past price information.

Specifically this book focuses on highly liquid markets (and so inefficiencies should be almost non-existent) and assumes a semi-strong form of the EMH (i.e. current prices reflect all-publicly available information). So, before we even start, the most important question we need to ask ourselves, "Is there any reason to be in the market for the technical traders in the first place"?

Well, the logical flaw of Random Walk Hypothesis is that traders have memories and they remember the past prices and those past prices help create the support and resistance levels of the market that influence their buying and selling decisions.

In the late 2004s, Scott H. Irwin and Cheol-Ho Park published a paper [4] which casts doubt on the Random Walk Hypothesis. They collected more than 100 empirical studies and reviewed how profitable those technical trading rules were. The results showed that technical analysis seems to work and also suggested a non-random and possibly predictive component to the future price movement.

So by applying proper technical analysis, we can identify those "predictive components" in the markets that might offer opportunities with some statistical edge and eventually provide something meaningful about the probabilities, which is the sole reason that any trader should be in the market.

Endnotes

[1] Charles Henry Dow (1851-1902), during the late nineteenth century, wrote in Wall Street Journal #255 editorial explaining his studies of the market dynamics based on price movements and trends formed by those movements. In 1932 Robert Rhea collected his works and published *The Dow Theory*.

[2] A Random Walk Down Wall Street, Burton Malkiel, New York: W.W. Norton, ©2015

[3] "Efficient Capital Markets: A Review of Theory and Empirical Work", Eugene Fama

[4] The Profitability of Technical Analysis: A Review; Department of Agricultural and Consumer Economics at the University of Illinois at Urbana Champaign, October 2004

Two

Swing Trading with Long and Short Positions

> *"Value Investing -The art of buying low and selling lower."* - Anonymous

With any trading instruments (like stock, ETF *[1]*, currency, commodity etc.), you can take two kind of trading positions: long or short.

If you take a long position, you are anticipating a rise in the value of the share price and you would experience a loss if the price falls. On the other hand, if you short (also called shorting or short selling) a stock, you are anticipating a fall in the value of the share price but if it actually rises, you would experience a loss, as shown in the figures below:

Trade	Profitable	Unprofitable
Long	Buy Low, Sell High	Buy High, Sell Low
Short	Sell High (first), Buy Lower (later)	Sell High, Buy Higher

Figure 2.1 a): Long and Short

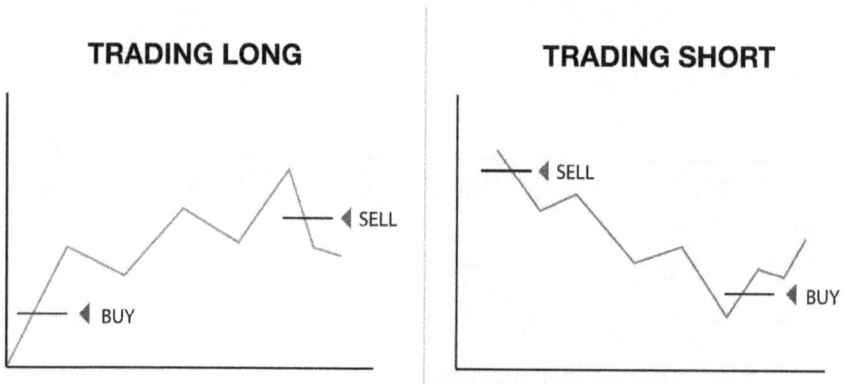

Figure 2.1 (b): Pictorial representation of Long and Short

When you trade short you want to sell high first and buy lower later as shown in Figure 2.1 a) and 2.1 b). Sell first and buy later is the important concept here as new traders often struggle with this concept, because it can seem absurd to sell shares first as you don't actually own it.

How do you sell something you don't own?

The action of selling something you don't own is facilitated through the use of margin (i.e. trading using leverage), which requires you to put up collateral to purchase the equities from a broker.

This is called the "initial margin", which is required to open up the short position and based upon the associated risk of the position solely determined by the broker.

For example, if you wanted to sell short of 10,000, Pier 1 Imports (PIR) shares at a price of $2.19 with an initial margin of 10%, you would be required to put up $2,190 as collateral.

10,000 * $2.19 = $21,900 (total cost of the position) * 10% = $2,190 (initial margin).

Let's assume you were right in your analysis and PIR continues to fall and you decide to exit the position at $1.01 and you have paid approximately $200 in brokerage to hold the position. Then your net profit equates to $11,600 (= ($2.19-$1.01)*10,000-$200).

Please note, after you put up the initial margin as security, you need to meet your daily obligations as well based on the revaluation of the position every day. That said, because your potential losses are not limited by the collateral you provide, if the position rises the broker will require you to put additional collateral to cover up your margin obligations. This is called the maintenance margin and you will receive a margin call from your broker to fulfill the obligation.

Failing to meet the maintenance margins can trigger forced liquidation where the brokerage automatically buys shares at the market price creating the hapless loss to the trader.

Moreover, cash flows, such as interest and dividends, are paid while the position is open, allowing price to track the underlying instrument. Therefore, when you open a short position, you will receive interest each day and (for dividend paying stocks) you have to pay any dividends on the ex-dividend date [2].

Market Structure and Principle of Price Behavior

Before we discuss about swing trading we need to discuss the market structure and principle of price behavior first as swing trading (or any other trading) is dependent upon these structures and principles.

Market Structure:

Technical traders structure the market based on the Third Dow Theorem [3]. It states that the market has three distinct phases and they are:

1. **Accumulation phase.** It is a period of price consolidation (ranging). The market is hesitant and the previous trend is depleted. The institutional superpowers feel some indecision in the market and build up the implementation of orders waiting to be executed.
2. **Absorption (mark up and mark down) phase.** As soon as the direction (uptrend or down trend) is approved, this phase begins. This becomes the pulse of the market in one direction or

the other; it is the massive influx of professional traders in the market creating the trend movement and pushing less capitalized retail investors to follow.

3. **Distribution phase.** This last phase is the phase for "correction" - when signs of instability appear, the big players take profits by closing their positions. While the novice small investors multiply their positions (in uptrend in euphoria and in downtrend in panic), the market is about to turn in the opposite trend. Price continues to move a little in the direction by inertia despite the absence of explicit prerequisites for this. But at the end, the opposite trend resumes.

See the diagram below:

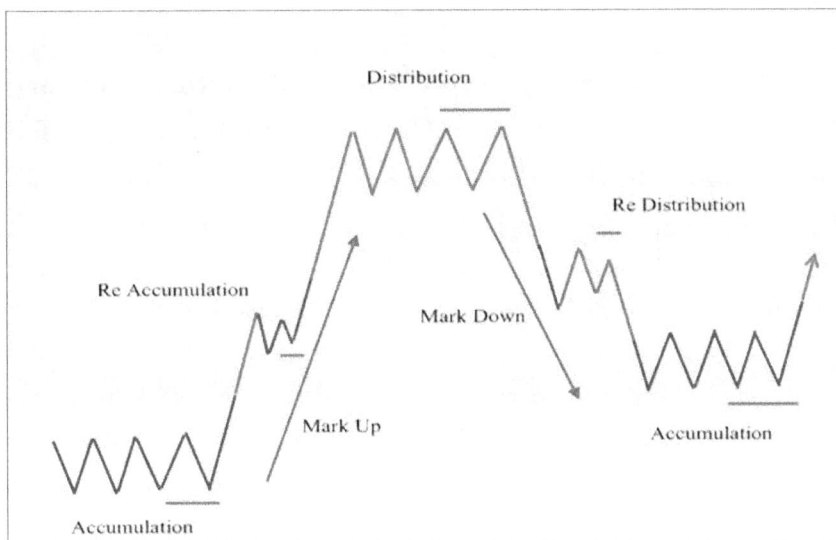

Figure 2.2 Market phases in Third Dow Theorem

Based on the market structure, only *four* types of trading are possible:

1. Trend (continuation) trading for uptrend or down trend

2. Breakout trading (price breaks the confine of a range and a new trend begins)
3. Range trading and
4. Reversal trading (from uptrend to downtrend and vice-versa)

Principle of Price Behavior:

There are four basic principles of price behavior which have held up over time. Confidence that a type of price action is a true principle is what allows a trader to develop a systematic approach. The following four principles can be modeled and quantified and hold true for all time frames, all markets. The majority of patterns or systems that have a demonstrable edge are based on one of these four enduring principles of price behavior.

1. A trend has a higher probability of continuation than reversal: One of the basic tenets of Dow Theory is that the market follows the Law of Inertia i.e. Newton's First Law of Motion *[4]* in trending market. Thus, if a financial instrument is trending, it tries to trend (theoretically) forever until substantial amount of force is exerted on it later to break the trend and to create a range or an opposite trend.

A major trend seldom reverses without warning, such as a pronounced loss of momentum followed by a period of accumulation or distribution, or a buying or selling climax.

In strong trends, reactions become shallower as the trend progresses.

The absence of any pattern in the price implies a continuation of the prevailing trend. The strongest trending action tends to be accompanied by a decrease in volatility.

Remember one Wall Street maxim: "Don't confuse brains with a bull (or bear) market" [5]. The directional moves in strong trends can be smooth and "trendy", which allows the trader to stay in long (for a bigger profit) and still manage the risk.

The anti-trend trading, in this case, will be like (I'll use another well-worn Wall Street adage here) "standing in front of a running freight train". This necessarily means, trader should be very alert in case of reversal trading.

Also, a strong trend is more forgiving of a sloppy entry as long as you enter in the right direction (so you can still exit with some profit).

Technically, in trend trading, an uptrend trader should buy at each retracement and should keep buying until the last retracement becomes a change of trend. Only in this trade she will lose money. (For simplicity, we are assuming here that, there will be no range formation during the re-accumulation phases of the trend.)

Similarly, the trader should sell in the downtrend at each retracement and should keep selling until the last retracement becomes a change of trend and only in this trade she would lose money. (For simplicity, we are also assuming here that, there will be no range formation during the re-distribution phases of the trend.)

Although this is an antithesis of our natural tendency to seek for "bargains" and "buy low / sell high", almost all floor traders buy when the price is high and sell when the price is low. See the example below:

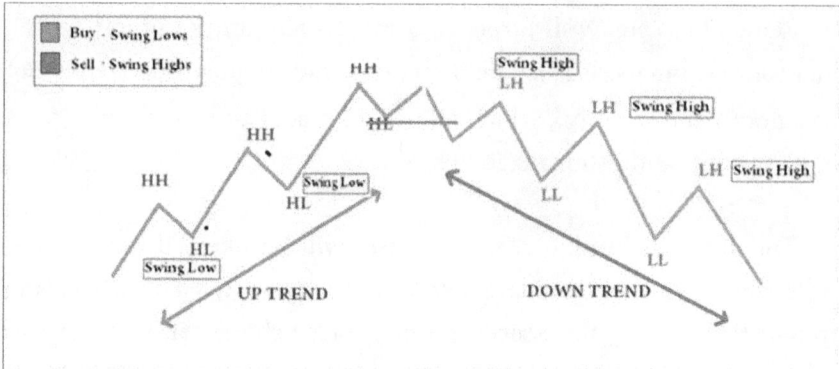

Figure. 2.3 Trend Trading

However, these are not the cases in range trading. In range trading, the market can be "choppy" and the trader can't stay in a trade for long as the price often changes directions at the confines.

2. Momentum precedes price: If momentum makes a new low or high, the price low or high is yet to come. Momentum is one of the few "leading" indicators. Ralph Nelson Elliot [6] used the term "impulse" to refer to an increase in momentum. Impulse indicates an imbalance in the supply and demand and often occurs in the direction of the prevailing trend.

Momentum can be defined using different types of oscillators like RSI [7], Stochastic etc. We will use Stochastic Oscillator as momentum oscillator throughout this book.

3. Trends end in a climax: A trend will continue until it reaches a "buying" or "selling" climax. Climax tends to be marked by an increase in volatility and volume. A buying or selling climax indicates that the last buyer or seller has been satisfied. The market then usually begins a process of re-tracing and re-testing, and in some cases, has a greater retracement to the opposite direction.

Trends tend to go further than we think they will and often, the price "overshoots" on the extremes. Price is at a new level and nobody has had a chance to get comfortable with the new levels. The market will tend to begin a testing process in both directions until it reaches a new equilibrium level. It is rare that a market immediately begins a sustained downtrend after it has been in an uptrend or vice-versa. The process of consolidating back to a new equilibrium point can be a long and drawn out process.

There is a very small percentage of time where a market makes a "V" or "inverse V (^)" spike reversal following a buying or selling climax. This is the most powerful pattern in technical analysis as it creates a vacuum to the other side. In these situations, the market sharply reverses its direction without the normal consolidation period. There must be both range expansion and an increase in volume followed by a sharp reaction in the opposite direction that forms what is commonly called a "tail".

Please see below the examples of V-bottom and V-top (or inverse V) type reversals:

Figure 2.4 a) V-Bottom Reversal
Courtesy: https://technicalresources.in

Figure 2.4 b) V-Top (or Inverse-V) Reversal
Courtesy: https://technicalresources.in

4. Market tends to alternate between a trending and non-trending (range/consolidation) environment: After a buying or selling climax, a trading range should begin. The "sideways line" (also called a coil) that forms when a market is going through after the buying or selling climax, gives the market potential energy for a larger move in the opposite direction.

What is swing trading?

Swing trading is a method of speculation which attempts to capture profit by the change in price or 'swing' of a financial instrument over a period of a few days to several months.

Identifying when to enter and exit a trade is the primary objective (and challenge) for swing traders and they may apply pure technical analysis (or a combination of fundamental and technical analysis) to identify the entry and exit points of the trade.

Swing trading is all about following the price action, learning how to enter trade with minimal risk and managing positions according to the markets' subsequent behavior. The last piece of information the market gives us is the one from which we need to make our next decision.

Professional swing trader is concerned with capitalizing on the short and intermediate price swings, and these are often caused by human emotions, such as fear and greed, in addition to change in supply and demand scenarios.

If the market is in a clearly defined trend, the largest price swings will occur in the direction of the trend. When the price is moving in a trend, many strategies could be found for entry based on the small retracements that occur along the way. These reactions allow the trader to find a minimal risk point while playing to the direction of the trend.

Monitoring the length and duration of a price swing relative to the previous swing sets the basic foundation for swing trading. Swing trading is nothing more than forecasting market move one "leg" or swing at a time. If the previous up-leg was greater than the previous down-leg (the retracement down was shallow), a trader would look to go long and vice-versa.

Swing trading is following the markets' most probable course of action and sticking to some important rules as below:

1. Determine the intermediate trend by observing whether the up-swings are greater than the downswings or vice versa. Figure 2.5 a) below represents an intermediate uptrend as 'a' (upswing) > 'c' (downswing). Similarly, 2.5 b) below represents an intermediate downtrend as 'c' (upswing) < 'a' (downswing). In a simplified model, we look to enter on retracements in the direction of the trend. Intermediate uptrend is identified when price action creates higher lows (HL) and higher highs (HH) [see Fig 2.5 a) below]. Similarly, intermediate downtrend is identified when price action creates lower lows (LL) and lower highs (HH) [see Fig 2.5 a) below].

2. The first price objective is the previous high in case of intermediate uptrend and previous low in case of intermediate downtrend.

3. Is the market making higher low (in case of uptrend) or lower high (in case of downtrend)? A higher low confirms support and a lower high confirms resistance. Figure 2.5 a) below represents an intermediate uptrend as higher lows (HL) have been formed. Similarly, 2.5 b) below represents an intermediate downtrend as lower highs (LH) have been formed.

4. What is the length of last swing relative to the previous swing? A shorter swing precedes a reversal. Longer swing denotes continuation and signals to enter on retracement. In figure 2.5 a) and 2.5 b) below: if 'b'> 'a', it denotes the continuation of respective trends otherwise indicates an upcoming reversal.

TRADING USING HIGHER HIGH & HIGHER LOW

Figure 2.5 a) Swing in a bullish trend

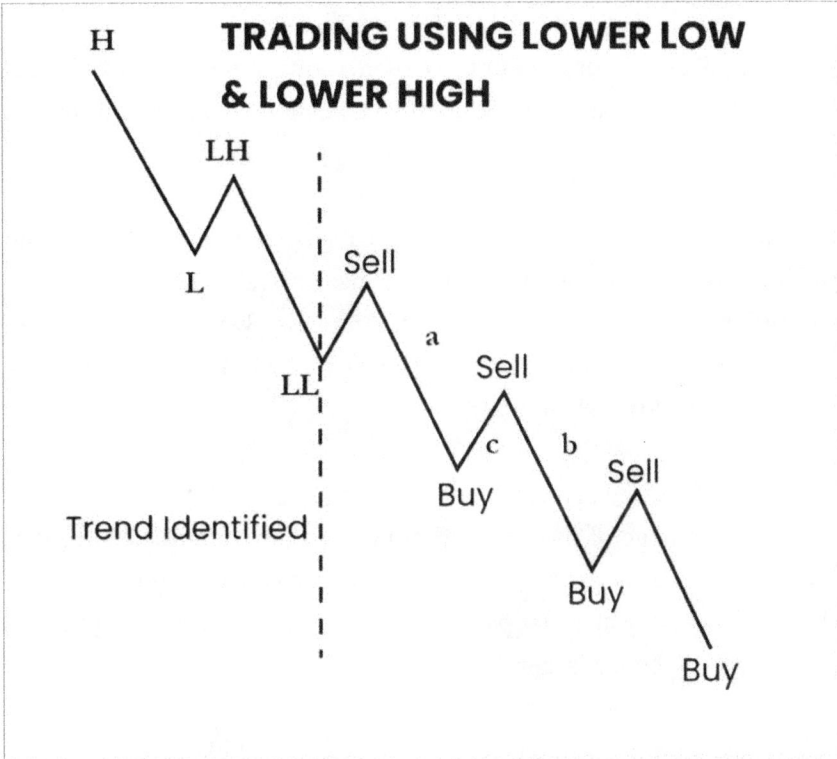

Figure 2.5 b) Swing in a bearish trend

5. In case of an intermediate bullish trend, the trend reversal is confirmed when the downswing length exceeds the upswing length. Similarly, in case of an intermediate bearish trend, when the upswing length exceeds the downswing length the trend reversal is confirmed.

6. **Downtrend swings tend to be sharper and faster than uptrend swings. Thus, when buying a lower low, exit more quickly. Conversely, when selling a higher high in uptrend, buy at the retracement.**

7. **Risk** should be defined by the last swing point. Always define your risk before entering a market. Never average a losing position and never add a second position to the short side.

8. Finally, if market loses swings or if they are small, do not trade.

Swing traders do not need perfect timing i.e. to buy at the very bottom and sell at the very top of price oscillations to make a profit. Small consistent earnings and compounding can generate substantial returns over time.

The majority of professional swing traders result in small wins and small losses; they nickel and dime the market week in and week out, and can make a consistent living in the process. Swing traders rely on a combination of two factors: numerous small winning trades and not letting a single loss gets too large.

Secondly, a large percentage of swing trading profits will come from a small percentage of the trades. A trader can't predict in advance that the market is ready to give a better than expected gain. Still, the trader should always stay alert yet patient, waiting for the market to give that one opening where a larger gain can be made.

Finally, approach the market with a directional bias. This does not necessarily mean that you have an opinion – only that you determine if there are higher probabilities of an market advance or decline. Are you looking to be a buyer or a seller?

Swing traders should select their candidates from the most actively traded stocks/ETF that show a tendency to swing within a broad, well-defined channel. It is necessary to keep a list of stocks/ETF and monitor them frequently and become familiar with the price action of those selected candidates. This is one of the core ideas of this book.

Endnotes

[1] Exchange Traded Fund (ETF): is a type of exchange traded investment product that must register with the U. S. Securities and Exchange Commission (SEC) under the 1940 Act as either a "fund" (i.e. an open-ended investment company) or a unit investment trust. Like mutual funds, ETF offers investors to pool their money in a fund that makes investments in stocks, bonds, or other assets and in return to receive an interest in that investment pool. Unlike mutual funds, however, ETF shares are traded on a national stock exchange and at market prices that may or may *not* be the same as the Net Asset Value (NAV) of the shares i.e. the value of the ETF's assets minus its liabilities divided by the number of shares outstanding.

[2] The ex-dividend date: is the trading date on and after which the dividend is not owed to a buyer of the stock. It is one business day before the date of record. The date of record is the day on which the company checks its records to identify shareholders of the company. An investor must be listed on that date to be eligible for a dividend payout.

[3] Third Dow Theorem: is based on third tenet of Dow Theory. Dow Theory is a foundational concept in technical analysis that provides a framework for ana-lyzing and interpreting stock market trends. It was developed by Charles H. Dow (1851-1902), one of the pioneers of modern financial journalism and the co-founder of Dow Jones & Company.

Dow Theory is based on the idea that the stock market moves in recognizable patterns and that these patterns can be analyzed to identify the current market trend and make predictions about future price movements. It focuses on the study of market indices, particularly the Dow Jones Industrial Average (DJIA) and the Dow Jones Transportation Average (DJTA), which Dow created himself.

The theory is built upon six basic tenets:

1. The market discounts everything: According to Dow Theory, the stock market reflects all available information, including fundamental factors, market psychology, and investor sentiment. Therefore, the prices of stocks already incorporate all known information.

2. The market moves in trends: Dow Theory asserts that the market tends to move in primary trends, which can be classified as either upward (bullish) or downward (bearish). These trends can persist for extended periods and provide opportunities for investors to profit.

3. **The primary trend has three phases: Dow Theory identifies three distinct phases within a primary trend. In an upward trend, these phases are accumulation (smart money buying), public participation (general public entering the market), and distribution (smart money selling). In a downward trend, they are called distribution, public participation, and panic selling.**

4. Indices should confirm each other: According to Dow Theory, for a trend to be considered valid, it should be confirmed by both the DJIA and the DJTA. In other words, if one index reaches a new high or low, the other index should ideally do the same. This principle helps analysts validate the strength and direction of a trend.

5. Volume should confirm the trend: Dow Theory suggests that trading volume should confirm the prevailing trend. In an uptrend, volume should expand as prices rise, indicating increased buying interest. Conversely, in a downtrend, volume should increase as prices decline, reflecting heightened selling pressure. Divergences between price and volume can indicate potential reversals.

6. Trends persist until proven otherwise: Dow Theory assumes that trends persist until sufficient evidence suggests otherwise. Therefore, traders and investors should assume that the current trend will continue until there are clear signals of a reversal.

Dow Theory provides a framework for market analysis and can be used to guide investment decisions. Technical analysts often employ various indicators, chart patterns, and Dow Theory principles to assess market trends, identify potential entry or exit points, and manage risk. However, it's important to note that Dow Theory is not foolproof, and like any investment methodology, it has its limitations and should be used in conjunction with other forms of analysis and risk management strategies.

[4] In 1686, in the "Principia Mathematica Philosophiae Naturalis", Sir Isaac Newton presented his first law of motion, which states that every object will remain at rest or in uniform motion (in a straight line) unless compelled to change its state by the action of an external force. This is also taken as the definition of inertia.

[5] This maxim is attributed to Humphrey Neill, founder of Contrary Opinion Forum in 1963

[6] Ralph N. Elliott, a professional accountant proposed the theory in the 1930's. He proposed that market prices unfold in specific patterns, which practitioners today call "Elliott waves" or simply "waves". Elliott published his theory of market behavior in the book *The Wave Principle* in 1938 and summarized it in a series of articles in *Financial World* magazine in 1939. The theory was popularized by Robert Prechter in the 1970's.

[7] Relative Strength Index (RSI): is a popular momentum oscillator and technical analysis tool used to measure the speed and change of price movements in financial markets. Developed by J. Welles Wilder Jr. in 1978, the RSI is widely employed by traders and investors to identify overbought and oversold conditions in a security, as well as to generate potential buy and sell signals.

The RSI is calculated using a mathematical formula that compares the magnitude of recent price gains to recent price losses. The index is expressed as a value ranging from 0 to 100, with readings above 70 typically indicating an overbought condition, while readings below 30 suggest an oversold condition. However, these threshold levels can be adjusted based on the specific characteristics of the market or security being analyzed. Please see the 14-period RSI diagram of a stock/ETF below:

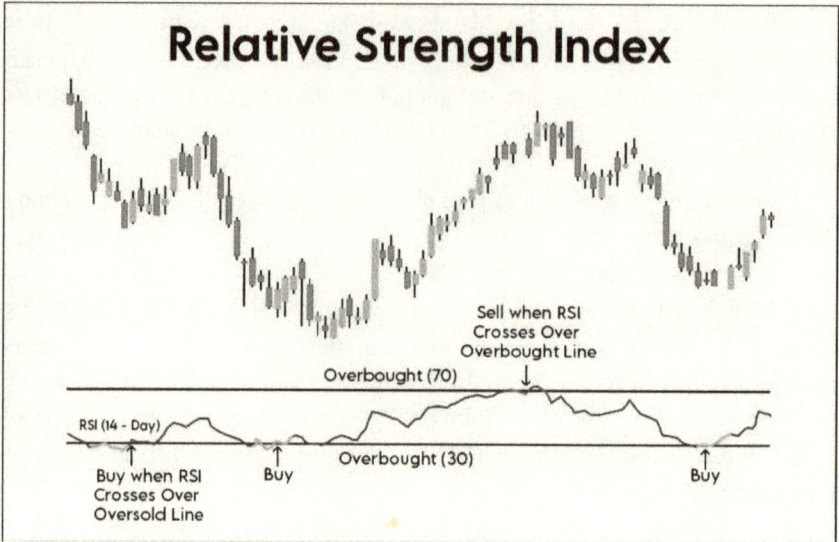

Relative Strength Index

Sell when RSI
Crosses Over
Overbought Line

Overbought (70)

RSI (14 - Day)

Overbought (30)

Buy when RSI
Crosses Over
Oversold Line

Buy

Buy

14 Period RSI of a Stock/ETF on Daily Chart

The formula for calculating the RSI involves several steps:

1. Determine the price change for a given period (default is 14, as suggested by Wilder): The RSI compares the magnitude of price gains and losses. To calculate the price change, subtract the previous closing price from the current closing price.
2. Calculate the average gain and average loss: The RSI typically considers a certain number of periods, default 14. Calculate the average gain by summing the gains over the selected periods and dividing by the number of periods. Likewise, calculate the average loss by summing the losses and dividing by the number of periods.
3. Calculate the relative strength (RS): The relative strength is the ratio of the average gain to the average loss. RS = Average Gain / Average Loss.
4. Calculate the RSI: The RSI is calculated using the following formula: RSI = 100 - (100 / (1 + RS)).

Once the RSI value is obtained, it can be plotted on a chart and used in various ways:

1. **Overbought and oversold levels:** Traders often consider RSI readings above 70 as indicating an overbought condition, suggesting that the price may be due for a reversal or a correction. Conversely, RSI readings below 30 are

commonly interpreted as oversold, implying that the price may be primed for a potential upward move.

2. **Divergence:** RSI divergence occurs when the price makes a new high or low, but the RSI fails to reach a corresponding high or low. This can signal a potential trend reversal or weakening of the current trend.

3. **RSI trend lines:** Traders sometimes draw trend lines on the RSI chart to identify patterns and potential breakouts or breakdowns. RSI trend line breakouts can confirm or foreshadow price trend changes.

4. **Bullish and bearish divergences:** Bullish divergence occurs when the price forms a lower low, while the RSI forms a higher low. This can indicate a potential bullish reversal. Conversely, bearish divergence occurs when the price forms a higher high, but the RSI forms a lower high, signaling a potential bearish reversal.

It's important to note that the RSI, like any technical indicator, has its limitations; false signals and whipsaws can occur, especially in choppy or sideways markets. Therefore, it's advisable to combine the RSI with other analysis techniques to increase the probability of accurate predictions and effective trading decisions.

This page is intentionally left blank

Three

Why Swing Trading?

> *"One of the funny things about the market is that every time one person buys, another sells and both think they are astute."* - William Feather

So far the trading time frame is concerned; there are three types of trading possible:

1. Intraday trading,
2. Swing trading and
3. Buy and hold (for long period like 20-25 years)

What is Intraday trading?

By definition, intraday trading or **day trading** is a form of speculation in securities in which the initiated position (either long or short) must be covered by the opposite position by the end of the trading day.

The day traders must go flat (meaning no buy or sell orders are open overnight) by the end of the day to avoid overnight market gyration (if any) and that's the underlying principle of day trading.

For example, one day trader went long (i.e. bought) with 10,000, Pier 1 Imports (PIR) shares at a price of $2.19 at the opening of a trading session. As the day progressed, it appeared that the overall market becoming bearish and PIR is trading below the buying price.

As the day trader must sell all 10,000 stocks during that session only to cover her position, she decided to take a loss and sold PIR at a price of $2.15 during the middle of the trading session. Her portfolio went flat by taking $400 loss (plus brokerage commission) to avoid overnight market gyration.

Please note that, should she kept the long position open instead and the market moved further south after hours and the price of PIR went below $2.15, she should have incurred more than $400 paper loss at the opening of the session next morning!

Most day traders lose money

Day traders have terrible track records. An academic paper published by three Brazilian economists Fernando Chague, Rodrigo De-Losso and Bruno Giovannetti in June 2020 [1] on the trading statistics of about 1,600 Brazilian day traders showed that 97% of them lost money over a period of 300 days.

Their conclusion: "We show that it is virtually impossible for individuals to day trade for a living, contrary to what course providers claim. We observe all individuals who began to day trade between 2013 and 2015 in the Brazilian equity futures market, the third in terms of volume in the world. We find that 97% of all individuals who persisted for more than 300 days lost money. Only 1.1% earned more than the Brazilian minimum wage and only 0.5% earned more than the initial salary of a bank teller — all with great risk."

A 2017 study on Taiwanese day traders [2] over a 15-year period, from 1992 to 2006 was conducted by University of California and Peking University, China concluded: "Less than 1% of the day trader population is able to predictably and reliably earn positive abnormal returns net of fees."

An older study in 2000 [3] also fared no better for day traders. Brad M. Barber and Terrance Odean of the University of California, Berkeley, analyzed 66,645 trading accounts at Charles Schwab from 1991 to 1996. They found that those who traded the most earned an annual return of 11.4%, while the market overall returned 17.9% during this interval. The authors thought that very active traders (they are most likely the day traders) seem to believe they know more than they really know. "Overconfidence can explain high trading levels and the resulting poor performance of individual investors. Our central message is that trading is hazardous to your wealth. Those who trade the most are hurt the most." the authors concluded, which echoes those of the other studies above.

People are free to trade their money any way they want, however these studies show that day trading is an uphill battle. Intraday-trading is hard and generally comes with **higher commission expenses** and with a **higher tax bill** than a long-term strategy. Also, the shorter the trading time frame is, the more it involves in taking massive concentrated risk in volatile assets. You might have success in day trading initially by sheer luck, but all it takes some bad trades to bury your accounts.

Successful traders with longevity ultimately discover a style that consistently works for them and the majority of the time that style does not involve intraday trading.

In this book, our objective is to come up with one of the best strategies which consistently make money and day trading should **not** be one of them as based on the conclusions of the studies above, it consistently lose money.

In the preceding chapter we've discussed about swing trading. Let's discuss now the benefits of swing trading over day trading below:

Benefits of swing trading over day trading

Although swing trading may expose the trades to the risk of market gyration by keeping the positions open overnights and the weekend (the price could gap down/up and the following sessions could open at substantially different prices), it still has tremendous benefits over the intraday trading:

1. Day traders have to compete with high-frequency traders, hedge funds, banks and other market professionals who spend millions to gain trading advantages. In this environment, a day trader has little choice but to spend heavily on a trading platform, advanced charting software, state-of-the-art computers, and the like.
2. Anyone with knowledge and trading capital can try swing trading. Because of the longer time frame (from days to months as opposed to minutes to hours), swing traders do not need to be glued to their computer screen all day. Swing trading can be done with just one computer and conventional trading tools. It does not require the state-of-the-art technology of day trading.

3. Day trading is an extremely stressful and expensive full-time job. Day traders must watch the market continuously during the day at their computer terminals. It's extremely difficult and demands great concentration to watch dozens of ticker quotes and price fluctuations to spot market trends. Also, this has to be done day after day, and the requirement for such a high degree of focus and concentration can often lead to burnout. Since day trading is intense and stressful, traders should be able to stay calm and control their emotions under fire. Swing trading, on the other hand, does not require such a formidable set of traits. Since swing trading is seldom a full-time job, there is much less chance of burnout due to stress. Swing traders usually have a regular job or another source of income from which they can offset or mitigate trading losses.

4. In day trading, ongoing expenses include costs for obtaining live price quotes and commission expenses that can be very high because of the volume of trades.

5. On the other hand, swing trade does not require live price quotes and as volume of trade is also very low compared to day trading, commission expenses are also much reasonable.

6. The biggest enemy of day traders is "time". Trades generally need time to work out. As the day trader must close the trade in a single session, if the market goes against the trade initially, the trade does not get sufficient time to "work" (i.e. market may change the direction later and favors the trade) and generally ends in hapless loss.

7. To the contrary in the case of swing trading, keeping a trade open for a few days or months may result in great profit even if the market does not favor the trade initially, however changes the course in time.

Now, let me discuss about the last trading method viz. buy and hold.

Buy and Hold

Ideally, buy and hold strategy should be categorized as an **investment method** and not as a trading method as in this strategy the assets are hold for longer period of time (at least 20 years) thus always long only. Also ideally, the portfolio under this strategy should consist of some tangible and hard assets like real estate, gold etc.

Issues with buy and hold strategy

A common saying between buy and hold investors is that, you need at least 20 year time horizon to come out ahead. However, there have been a number of 20-year rolling periods during which the market performance was very weak or negative, factoring in the inflation.

During this 20-year period an investor is exposed to *all* bear market and black-swan events. As you never take profits during this buy and hold period, you will *keep giving the profit back time and again.* From figure 3.1 below, look at the yo-yo market from the peak in March 2000 to the bottom in October 2002 and again from the peak in October 2007 to the bottom in March 2009:

SP - S&P 500 Index (IOM) - Monthly OHLC Chart

Fig. 3.1 S&P monthly chart from 1997 to 2011
Image credit: Barchart.com

In bear market, ordinary buy-and-hold investors, hold equities on for dear life, hoping and praying that the market rebounds. Even when the market recovers no one knows how long it will take just to get back to the previous market highs as it can take many years to get back even.

Thus for these novice buy-and-hold investors down market cause panic, pain and incorrect decision making. In general, these uninformed investors *sell* at market *bottoms* (in fear) and *buy* at market *tops* (in euphoria), unintentionally killing their chances of making back the losses on the eventual recovery of the market.

Preservation of Capital is paramount in any investing plan; however as buy-and-hold strategy is only *practical* in bull market, it offers no plan to protect money as the market trends downward. Warren Buffett, one of the most successful and well known investors of all time and a proponent of buy-and-hold investing was not immune from the financial crisis and stock market mauling; Berkshire Hathaway's Class A equities fell over 53% dropping from a peak of $148,900 on December 11, 2007 to a bottom of $73, 195 on March 09, 2009.

Criticism on swing trading method

Based on the discussion above it is clear that, in swing trading we try to pick the low and high points of the market to buy and sell respectively and do it in iteration. However the buy-and-hold club criticizes that, the commission and taxes will eat away at the principal in this strategy.

Answer to this criticism is that, commissions for buying and selling ETFs (or stocks) have dropped significantly in the past few years. Using some discount brokers, an investor can even trade with **zero** commission and for many other brokers the cost could be less than $10. As of writing the list of zero commission brokers is substantial: Charles Schwab, Fidelity Investments, JP Morgan Chase (self-directed investing), Merrill Edge, Ally Financial, Vanguard Group, TD Ameritrade, E-trade, Interactive Brokers etc. Thus commission is *not* a cost prohibiting factor for the retail investors.

So far the tax is concerned the buy-and-hold investors also have no immunity to it. Buy-and-hold club proposes a diversified portfolio of individual stocks, bonds and mutual funds which will (supposedly) provide positive returns over long time frames. Mutual funds do pass on capital gains at year end to the investors and on which they must pay taxes for that tax year.

It is true that, investors do not pay taxes on individual stocks and bonds until they are sold; however individual stocks and bonds **risks** are more dreaded than paying taxes as the former can wipe out an entire portfolio. In long only swing trading method with ETF only, the individual stocks and bonds risks are non-existent.

Thus in any event, this entire argument from buy-and-hold investors is bogus.

Endnotes

[1] Day Trading for a Living? By Fernando Chague and Bruno Giovannetti, Getulio Vargas Foundation (FGV) - Sao Paulo School of Economics; Rodrigo De-Losso, University of São Paulo (USP) - Department of Economics (Last revised: 15 Jun 2020)

[2] Do Day Traders Rationally Learn About Their Ability? By Brad M. Barber - Graduate School of Management University of California Davis; Yi-Tsung Lee, Yu-Jane Liu - Guanghua School of Management Peking University China; Terrance Odean, Ke Zhang - Haas School of Business University of California Berkeley (Last revised: October 2017)

[3] Trading Is Hazardous to Your Wealth: The Common Stock Investment Performance of Individual Investors by Brad M. Barber - Graduate School of Management University of California, Davis; Terrance Odean - Haas School of Business University of California, Berkeley (Last revised: April 2000)

Four

Why trade ETFs only and no individual stocks?

> *"The market may be bad, but I slept like a baby last night. I woke up every hour and cried"* - Anonymous.

In this chapter we are going to propose to invest *only* in Exchange Traded Funds (ETF) and not in stocks as investing in individual stocks could be a risky proposition.

Individual companies can go bust if there is inept management, financial or accounting scandals, decreased company earnings or outside factors impacting the ability to make profit. In Wall Street [1] many stocks can also go out of favor for no reasons for a prolonged period of time.

Examples for those risky stocks even could be the number of "supposedly" blue-chip stocks that have gone bankrupt, have merged or acquired (because of bad performances) or the share price dropped to single digit in recent years. Dow Jones Industrial Average (^DJIA), a collection of thirty blue-chip stocks, has had to replace various stocks over the years due to poor financial performances or mergers or acquisition.

In today's interconnected digital economy, which moves in lightning speed with internet and cellular phones, rumors and false information about an individual stock can spread just as quickly and can knock down the price from 10-25% even though that drop was not warranted. Even when some real information like an after-hours earning announcement hits the internet stating that a stock's earning is not in line with analysts' estimate, the price of it could drop easily 10% to 25% within minutes.

From the discussion above, investing in individual stocks indeed could be a risky proposition and diversification among asset classes through bundle of stocks is necessary and is a cornerstone of investing.

ETFs solve this purpose and specific ETFs could be used as investment vehicles of choice instead of individual stocks (as defined earlier, an ETF is a collection of hundreds of stocks in a single fund that trades on major stock exchanges).

Moreover, ETF could be used in lieu of Fixed Income securities (like corporate, municipal and treasury bonds), Currencies (like USD, Euro, Yen etc.) and Commodities (like corn, wheat, soybean etc.)

ETF benefits are significant and extensive

- As ETFs are traded in exchanges like regular stocks, any investing or trading strategy can be applied to it

- Liquidity: ETFs are very liquid and can be bought/sold in trading hours like individual stocks using market, limit or stop orders [2]
- Tax-efficiency: In ETF, minimal transaction and portfolio turnover are necessary; thus the capital gain distribution is minimal
- Use of margin: Although, **most investors should avoid margin**, ETF could be traded on margin like ordinary stocks. Please note, Mutual Funds [3] could not be bought on margin.
- Dividend income: There are many ETFs provide regular dividends.
- Volatility: ETF volatility could be much lower compared to the volatility of constituent individual equities.
- (Synthetic) shorting by going long: One of the most interesting features of ETF is that, you can synthetically short the market by buying (i.e. going long) the *inverse* ETF. This is a simpler operation than shorting and there is also no margin interest charges as the inverse ETFs are bought long.
- Bear market profits can be made by purchasing inverse ETFs as they rise when the market falls. Inverse ETFs can also be used as a hedge in portfolio in a rising market: it acts like insurance should the market fall.

Risks associated with leveraged ETF

A leveraged ETF generally tracks a market index or asset class, and uses debt (i.e. leverage) to boost the fund's return and hence the name.

A leveraged ETF holds both debt and shareholder equity, uses the debt to amplify the daily return to shareholders. Non-leveraged ETF, by contrast, holds only shareholder equity and simply track an underlying index or asset class with the goal of matching that index or asset's performance. Leveraged ETFs aim to generate daily returns that are multiples (like 1.5, 2 or 3 times) of the performance of the underlying index or asset class with the objective of earning returns that exceed the cost of assuming the debt (for example interest on debt, options premium etc.).

Leveraged ETFs may also use derivatives (such as swaps, options and/or futures contracts) to amplify returns. Inverse leveraged ETFs use derivatives to generate the *opposite* of the daily return of an index or asset class. Thus if S&P 500 falls 10% in one day, S&P 500 3X ETF will fall 30% and S&P 500 *inverse* 2X ETF will rise 20%.

The issues and risks associated with the leveraged ETFs are as below:

1. Leveraged ETFs do not mirror the return of underlying index or asset class

Because of the compounding effect of leverage over time, the long-term returns generated by leveraged ETFs do not simply mirror the returns of the index or asset class they are designed to track. Consider the following example:

The trailing one-year performance of 3 ETFs viz. QQQ (Invesco QQQ trust – a regular NASDAQ 100 index ETF), TQQQ (ProShares UltraPro QQQ - an ETF with 3x leveraged exposure to NASDAQ 100 index) and SQQQ (ProShares UltraPro Short QQQ - an ETF with -3x (i.e. *inverse*) leveraged exposure to NASDAQ 100 index) is as in Figure 4.1 below:

Fig. 4.1 Trailing one year performance of QQQ, TQQQ and SQQQ
Image credit: Stockcharts.com

Over the trailing year, TQQQ has provided a little over 3x return to QQQ's gain. However, SQQQ has fallen by just over twice the amount of QQQ's gain.

2. Adverse effect of volatility in leveraged ETFs

For periods under which the market tends to be under stress and more volatile, leveraged ETFs are very likely to be off the mark when used over long period of time.

For example, as in Figure 4.2 below, during the period of COVID-19 pandemic starting March 2020, all three of these ETFs notched negative returns. QQQ fell by 11.2% for the month, meaning that, theoretically inverse ETF (SQQQ) should have resulted in a gain. However, SQQQ fell by 5.9% during this time frame and TQQQ was down by over 4 times (albeit theoretically it should go down exactly 3 times):

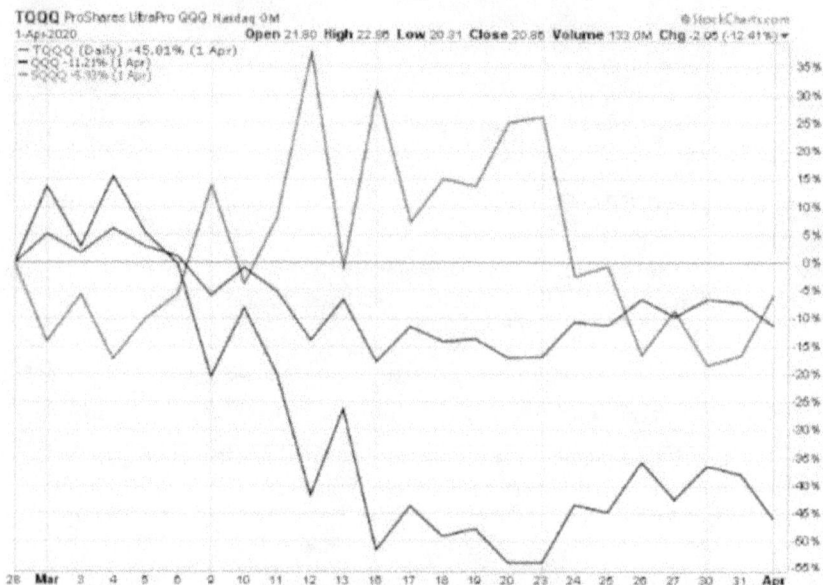

Fig. 4.2 Effect of market volatility on QQQ, TQQQ and SQQQ
Image credit: Stockcharts.com

3. Derivative risks

As mentioned earlier, besides debt, leveraged ETFs may also use derivatives (such as swaps, options and/or futures contracts) to amplify returns. Derivatives are investment instruments that consist of agreements between parties. Their value depends on the price of an underlying financial asset. The primary risks associated with trading derivatives are market, counterparty, liquidity and interconnection risks [4]. Investing in leveraged ETFs indirectly exposes investors to all of these risks.

4. Daily reset and constant leverage trap

Leveraged ETFs reset to their underlying benchmark index or asset class on a daily basis to maintain a fixed leverage ratio. That is *not* at all how traditional margin accounts work and this resetting process results in a situation known as constant leverage trap.

For example, consider a 2X leveraged ETF fund has $100 million of assets and has taken $100 million of debt (leverage) to make $200 million of index exposure. The index rises 1% on the first day of trading, giving the firm $2 million in profits (assuming no expenses for simplicity). The fund now has $102 million of assets and then must take **an extra $2 million of debt** to double its index exposure to $204 million. So, even if the fund profited, it has to take a new loan to maintain the daily ratio of 2X and this represents the situation of constant leverage trap.

5. Expensive exposure

Along with the risk of performance not being in line with expectations, leveraged ETFs also charge a higher management fee to accommodate the expense of leveraging and daily rebalancing of the funds. While cost is unlikely to be a factor in selecting leveraged ETFs, it is still a factor that contributes to the erosion of performance over time.

Relative to its vanilla counterpart QQQ, TQQQ is nearly five times as expensive (see Figure 4.3 below):

QQQ vs TQQQ Costs

Expense Ratio	Expense Ratio
0.20%	0.95%
Average Spread (%)	Average Spread (%)
0.00%	0.01%
Average Spread ($)	Average Spread ($)
$0.01	$0.01

Fig. 4.3 Comparison of management fees QQQ vs. TQQQ
Image credit: FactSet.com

6. Leveraged ETFs may go to zero

As explained above, leveraged ETF prices tend to decay over time and as a result, they can tend toward zero. Before this happens, leveraged ETFs can undertake a reverse ETF split, creating higher-priced shares but reducing the number of ETF units outstanding. Ultimately, if the share prices drop low enough and there is no demand for a reverse split, the ETF may be delisted.

Since they maintain a fixed level of leverage, leveraged ETF may even collapse in a single day. For example, 3x ETFs may face complete collapse if the underlying index declines more than 33% on a single day.

7. Issues with liquidity

Some leveraged ETFs are not heavily traded, meaning that your ability to buy or sell shares may be constrained. For example, as of writing although SQQQ holds over $1.74 billion in assets, its trading volume is much lower compared to QQQ, which means the spread is higher than that of its counterpart QQQ.

Conclusion: Based on the issues and risks associated with the leveraged ETFs discussed above, we should all together avoid them as investment/trading vehicle in this book.

Endnotes

[1] Wall Street is an eight block long street running between Broadway in the west and South Street/East River in the east and situated in the Financial District of Lower Manhattan in New York City. The term "Wall Street" has become a metonym for the New York based financial markets as a whole and the Financial District itself.

Wall Street was originally known in Dutch as "de Waal Straat" when it was part of New Amsterdam, a Dutch settlement established in the 17th century at the southern tip of Manhattan Island. During that period, Wall Street was a slave trading marketplace and also a securities trading site. Interestingly, a wooden wall existed on the street from 1685 to 1699.

[2] Market, limit and stop order: A <u>market order</u> is an order to buy or sell a security at the market's current best available price. It typically ensures immediate execution, but does not guarantee a specified price.

A stock quote typically includes the highest bid (for sellers), lowest offer (for buyers), and the last trade price. However, the last trade price may not necessarily be current, particularly in a fast-moving market when stock prices can change significantly in a short period of time.

Therefore, when placing a market order, the current bid and offer prices are of greater importance than the last trade price. Market order is appropriate if you want to fill your buy order or execute your sell order immediately without thinking about price guarantee over the last traded price.

<u>Example</u>: The market is open and the last trade price of IBM stock was $261. If we place a buy market order now (provided no unusual market conditions are present) it will be executed immediately at the lowest ask price (which will be at or slightly above the stock's current price of $261).

To the opposite, if you want to sell some IBM stock that you have and placed a sell market order now (provided no unusual market conditions are present) it will be executed immediately at the highest bid price (which will be at or slightly below the stock's current price of $261).

Limit order: A limit order is an order to buy or sell a security with a restriction on the maximum price to be paid or the minimum price to be received (the "limit price"). If the order is filled, it will only be at the specified limit price or better. However, there is no guarantee of execution. A limit order may be appropriate when you think you can buy at a price lower than or sell at a price higher than the current price.

Example: The last trade price of IBM stock was $261. Your analysis says that the price of IBM stock will drop below the present price to $250 soon and so that you can buy it at a cheaper price later. You place a Good-Till-Canceled (GTC) buy limit order of IBM stocks for $250. If your analysis was correct, it will be executed sometimes in near future otherwise no execution will occur.

To the opposite, you have some IBM stock and your analysis says that the price of it will rise above the present price to $270 soon and so that you can sell it at a higher price later. You place a Good-Till-Canceled (GTC) sell limit order of IBM stocks for $270. If your analysis was correct, it will be executed sometimes in near future otherwise no execution will occur.

Stop order: A stop order is an order to buy or sell a security at the market price once it has traded at or through a specified price (the "stop price"). If the security reaches the stop price, the order becomes a market order and is filled at the next available market price. If the security fails to reach the stop price, the order is not executed. A stop order may be appropriate in the following scenarios:

1. When a stock you own (/sold short) has risen (/fell further) and you want to protect your gain should it begin to fall (/rise) again or
2. You want to buy (/sell) a stock as it breaks out above (/below) a certain resistance (/support) level, believing that it will continue to rise (/fall).

A stop order is also referred to as a "stop-loss" order as it helps to minimize a loss. A "stop loss" order may be appropriate when you are directionally wrong and to prevent further loss forced to sell security at a price lower than the purchase price or buy back at a price higher than the price you shorted the security.

Example: The last trade price of IBM stock was $261. Your analysis says that the price of IBM stock will drop below the present price to $250 soon and so that you shorted the stock at this price. Your analysis also says that, IBM stock will not go over $270 in near term. However to be on the safer side if you were directionally wrong, you place a GTC buy stop order for $271. If IBM ever reaches the stop price in near term, the order becomes a market order and is filled at the next available market price.

Now to the opposite scenario, your analysis says that the price of IBM stocks will go up to $270 soon and you bought the stocks at the present price of $261. Your analysis also says that, IBM stock will not go below $250 in near term. However to be on the safer side if you were directionally wrong, you place a GTC sell stop order for $249. If IBM ever reaches the stop price in near term, the order becomes a market order and is filled at the next available market price.

[3] Mutual Funds: A mutual fund is an SEC-registered open-end investment company that pools money from investors and invests in stocks, bonds, money market funds, other assets or combination of these investments. The combined assets and securities the mutual fund owns are known as "portfolio", which is managed by an SEC-registered investment adviser. Unlike ETF, Mutual Funds are not exchange traded.

Each mutual fund share represents an investor's proportionate ownership of the portfolio and the income it generates. Investors in mutual fund buy their shares from and redeem their shares to the fund themselves. Mutual funds are required by law to price their shares each business day and they typically do so after the major U.S. exchanges close. This price, fund asset values minus its liabilities per share is called the Net Asset Value (NAV).

[4] Market, counterparty, liquidity and interconnection risks: Market risk in Finance is defined as a risk (possibility) that, entities may experience losses investing or trading due to the factors that affect the overall performance of the market. These factors include changes in interest rates or exchange rates, economic recession, geo-political events, black swan events etc. Market risk cannot be eliminated through diversification however could be hedged through (Put) Options, Index Options or using Volatility Index (VIX).

Counterparty risk (also referred as default risk) is a risk that, your counterparty in a transaction cannot honor its obligation to you. In derivative market every trade needs to have two parties to take the opposite sides. This risk is higher in

Over-the-Counter (OTC) markets, which are much less regulated than ordinary trading exchanges.

For example, some equity put options has been bought in OTC market. Now, if the market plunges, the Mark to Market (MTM) value of the put options increases sharply, introducing significant counterparty risk to the buyer of the put options as the seller of the put options may default in this case (MTM process facilitates contract performance by requiring margin deposits that are adjusted daily). Similar risk exists in swaps and other derivatives like futures.

Liquidity risk applies to investors who plan to close out derivative trades prior to maturity. Such investors need to consider the possibility that, it will be difficult to liquidate (close out) the trades if existing bid-ask spreads become so large to represent a significant cost.

Interconnection risk: Financial interconnectedness is the network of credit exposures, trading and other relationships and dependencies between financial agents. Financial agents could be (i) financial institutions (banks and non-banks), (ii) providers of financial market infrastructure services and (iii) vendors and third parties supporting these entities. For example, contractual obligations among financial institutions (such as ownership, loans, derivatives and many other types of contracts) create interconnectedness between them.

Interconnectedness matters because it serves as a conduit for contagion. In a highly interconnected financial system, distress in one entity is likely to be transmitted to other entities. These interconnections have proven to propagate shocks beyond their original impact, amplifying them in the process. The global financial crisis in 2008 that unfolded in the wake of the Lehman Brothers insolvency was a dramatic example of this phenomenon.

This page is intentionally left blank

Five

Which ETF classes to consider?

> *"The four most dangerous words in investing are, it's different this time."* -Sir John Templeton

According to the Global Industry Classification Standard (GICS) system, the following market sectors have been defined:

1. Energy
2. Materials
3. Industrials
4. Utilities
5. Healthcare
6. Financials
7. Consumer Discretionary
8. Consumer Staples

9. Information Technology
10. Communication Services and
11. Real Estate

First and foremost, we will select ETFS based on these 11 sectors. To provide further diversifications, we will also consider other ETFs based on the following asset classes as below:

- Bond fund ETFs and "treasury" ETFs (on T-notes, T-bill etc.)
- Broad based Index ETFs (on DJIA, S&P500, Russel 2000 etc.)
- Currency ETFs (on USD, Euro, British Pound Sterling etc.)
- Cryptocurrency ETF (on Bitcoin)
- Geography based ETFs (on Emerging markets)
- Commodity based ETFs (on Gold, Silver, Oil, Natural Gas etc.)
- Volatility index based ETFs (on S&P volatility index, NASDAQ 100 volatility index etc.)

The set of ETFs in 11 sectors plus the other set of ETFs under the asset classes mentioned above will provide the broad spectrum of assets which are also properly diversified. Below we provide the complete list of these ETFs:

No.	ETF Type	Ticker Symbol	Description	Remark
1	Sector	XLP	Consumer Staples Select Sector SPDR Fund	

2	Sector	XLV	Health Care Select Sector SPDR Fund
3	Sector	XLI	Industrial Select Sector SPDR Fund
4	Sector	XLK	Technology Select Sector SPDR Fund
5	Sector	XLY	Consumer Discretionary Select Sector SPDR Fund
6	Sector	XLU	Utilities Select Sector SPDR Fund
7	Sector	XLE	Energy Select Sector SPDR Fund
8	Sector	XRT	SPDR S&P Retail ETF
9	Sector	IYR	iShares U.S. Real Estate ETF

10	Sector	XLF	Financial Select Sector SPDR Fund	
11	Sector	XOP	SPDR S&P Oil & Gas Exploration & Production ETF	Coming under "Energy" sector
12	Sector	XBI	SPDR S&P Biotech ETF	Coming under "Healthcare" sector
13	Sector	KRE	SPDR S&P Regional Banking ETF	Coming under "Financial" sector
14	Broad based index	QQQ	Invesco QQQ Trust	Based on NASDAQ-100 Index
15	Broad based index	IWM	iShares Russell 2000 ETF	
16	Broad based index	DIA	SPDR Dow Jones Industrial Average ETF Trust	

17	Broad based index	SPY	SPDR S&P 500 ETF Trust	
18	Bonds/ Treasury Securities	TLT	iShares 20+ Year Treasury Bond ETF	
19	Bonds/ Treasury Securities	IEF	iShares 7-10 Year Treasury Bond ETF	
20	Bonds/ Treasury Securities	HYG	iShares iBoxx $ High Yield Corporate Bond ETF	
21	Bonds/ Treasury Securities	LQD	iShares iBoxx $ Investment Grade Corporate Bond ETF	
22	Bonds/ Treasury Securities	EMB	iShares J.P. Morgan USD Emerging Markets Bond ETF	Also belongs to "Emerging Markets" ETF group

23	Emerging Markets	FXI	iShares China Large-Cap ETF
24	Emerging Markets	ASHR	Xtrackers Harvest CSI 300 China A-Shares ETF
25	Emerging Markets	EFA	iShares MSCI EAFE ETF
26	Emerging Markets	EEM	iShares MSCI Emerging Markets ETF
27	Emerging Markets	EWJ	iShares MSCI Japan ETF
28	Emerging Markets	EWZ	iShares MSCI Brazil ETF
29	Emerging Markets	KWEB	KraneShares CSI China Internet ETF

30	Volatility	VIX	iPath Series B S&P 500 VIX Short-Term Futures ETN [1]	
31	Currency	UUP	Invesco DB US Dollar Index Bullish Fund	
32	Crypto-currency	BITO	Pro-Shares Bit-coin Strategy ETF	
33	Com-modity	SLV	iShares Silver Trust	
34	Com-modity	GLD	SPDR Gold Shares	
35	Com-modity	GDX	VanEck Gold Miners ETF	
36	Com-modity	USO	United States Oil Fund, LP	Also comes under "Energy" sector
37	Com-modity	UNG	United States Natu-ral Gas Fund, LP	Also comes under "Energy" sector

38	Miscellaneous	SMH	VanEck Semiconductor ETF
39	Miscellaneous	JETS	U.S. Global Jets ETF
40	Miscellaneous	ARKK	ARK Innovation ETF

Selection criteria for these ETFs

Any running list of financial products is "theoretically" outdated even at the time of writing, as the list can change dynamically with the inclusion of new product(s) or exclusion of any existing product. Thus, we need to provide the selection criteria of these ETFs so that, if need be readers can develop the list on their own based on the criteria:

1. ETFs will be fairly liquid with at least one (1) million trading volume per day.
2. ETFs must be optionable (discussed later).
3. The price of the ETFs must be greater than or equal to $5 (We don't want to consider very low priced ETFs. If an ETF price is very low, there must have been underlying negative reason(s) responsible for that; generally these ETFs are candidates for shorting and which is against the principle of this book).

These three conditions above can be satisfied using the following filters in Finviz.com "Screener" page (https://finviz.com/screener.ashx):

Industry = "Exchange Traded Fund", Current Volume ="Over 1M", Option/Short="Optionable", Price="Over $5"

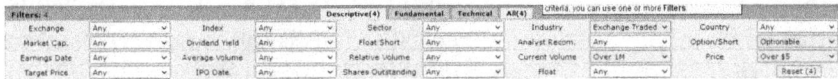

Fig. 5.1 Filters on ETF selection under Finviz.com "Screener" tab

4. ETFs will be the member of CBOE [2] "Penny Interval Program". The Penny Interval Program allows some stocks, ETFs and indexes to trade their related options in increments of $0.01. The minimum price increment of premiums for series of options included in the Penny Interval Program will be $0.01, while the strike price is below $3.00 and $0.05 while the strike price is above $3.00. However, the minimum increment of premiums for all option series in QQQ, IWM and SPY is $0.01 irrespective of the strike prices.

At the time of writing CBOE lists only the top 373 most actively traded stocks, ETFs and index option classes in the Penny Interval Program. The latest list for the same can be obtained from the following link: https://www.nasdaq.com/docs/2020/12/31/PennyProgram-Jan2021.xlsx

The difference between the bid (selling) and ask (buying) price (also called the spread) could be notoriously large in options. While selling the put (discussed later) or covered call (also discussed later) if the spread is very high, the chance of getting a very low selling price is also very high.

The penny interval program was initiated by the SEC was to reduce trading costs for investors by reducing the potential for market makers to earn a larger spread between option prices thereby allowing investors to trade options at better prices.

As the increment of premiums in Penny Interval Program is very low ($0.01 and $0.05), the spread between the bid and ask price is also very low in general. This ensures us we get a fairly priced selling price while selling puts or covered calls. This is the reason we want to ensure that, the ETFs in our list is a member of CBOE "Penny Interval Program".

Endnotes

[1] Exchange Traded Notes (ETN): is a senior (In finance, senior note is a debt that takes priority over other unsecured or otherwise more "junior" debt owed by the issuer. In the event the issuer goes bankrupt, senior debt theoretically must be repaid before other creditors receive any payment. Senior debt is often secured by collateral on which the lender has put in place a first lien.), unsecured, unsubordinated debt security issued by an underwriting bank. Similar to other debt securities, ETNs have a maturity date and are backed only by the credit of the issuer.

ETNs are designed to provide investors access to the returns of various market benchmarks (like market indexes). When an investor buys an ETN, the underwriting bank promises to pay the amount reflected in the index, minus fees upon maturity. Thus ETN has an additional risk compared to an ETF; if the credit of the underwriting bank becomes suspect, the investment might lose value in the same way that a senior debt would. ETNs are usually traded on an exchange and can be sold short; ETNs do not actually own any underlying assets of the indexes or benchmarks they are designed to track.

The first ETN was developed and issued in May 2000 in Israel by Haim Even-Zahav the CEO of Psagot-Ofek financial instruments of Leumi group under the product name TALI-25.

[2] The Chicago Board Options Exchange (CBOE), located at 433 West Van Buren Street in Chicago, IL is the largest U.S. options exchange. As of writing, CBOE offers options on over 2,200 companies, 22 stock indexes and 140 ETFs. The Chicago Board of Trade established the Chicago Board Options Exchange in 1973. The CBOE is regulated by the Securities and Exchange Commission (SEC) and owned by CBOE Global Markets.

This page is intentionally left blank

Six

Introduction to Options

> *"I put two children through Harvard by trading options. Unfortunately, they were my broker's children."* – Jason Zweig

What are Options?

Options are financial contracts, which give the options **buyer** the **right** to **buy** or **sell** an underlying asset at a fixed price, on or before a specified future date. The underlying assets may include stocks, indexes, ETFs, fixed income products, currencies or commodities etc.

The fixed price is called the **Strike Price** and the specified future date is called the **Expiry Date** of that option. After the expiry date, the whole options dissolve and become worthless; thus options are temporally decaying or "wasting" (i.e. depreciating) assets.

Options are also **derivatives** as their prices are *derived* from an underlying asset. The prices of the options are also called the **Premiums** for the options.

In general, two types of options are traded viz. **Call** and **Put** options. Call option provides the buyer the right to **buy** the underlying asset at a strike price, on or before the expiry date of the options. And Put option provides the buyer the right to **sell** the underlying asset at a strike price, on or before the expiry date of the options.

As a real life example, below is the list of options (also called the "**Options chain**") for BITO, the ProShares Bitcoin Strategy ETF, with the **Expiry Date** of October 21, 2022:

Calls			Strike	Puts		
Bid	**Mid**	**Ask**	**Strike**	**Bid**	**Mid**	**Ask**
11.00	11.08	11.15	**1.00**	-	-	0.03
10.00	10.07	10.15	**2.00**	-	0.01	0.01
9.00	9.05	9.10	**3.00**	-	-	0.05
8.00	8.07	8.15	**4.00**	-	0.01	0.03
7.00	7.05	7.10	**5.00**	0.01	0.03	0.04
6.00	6.08	6.15	**6.00**	0.03	0.04	0.05
5.05	5.15	5.25	**7.00**	0.06	0.08	0.09
4.00	4.13	4.25	**8.00**	0.11	0.13	0.14
3.20	3.25	3.30	**9.00**	0.22	0.23	0.23
2.36	2.44	2.52	**10.00**	0.38	0.39	0.40
1.61	1.66	1.70	**11.00**	0.63	0.65	0.67
1.08	1.09	1.09	**12.00**	1.05	1.06	1.07
			Last: 12.06			
0.65	0.67	0.68	**13.00**	1.62	1.64	1.66
0.37	0.39	0.41	**14.00**	2.34	2.37	2.39
0.23	0.24	0.25	**15.00**	3.15	3.20	3.25
0.13	0.15	0.16	**16.00**	4.05	4.10	4.15
0.08	0.10	0.11	**17.00**	5.00	5.08	5.15
0.07	0.08	0.08	**18.00**	5.95	6.03	6.10
0.02	0.05	0.07	**19.00**	6.95	7.03	7.10
0.02	0.04	0.05	**20.00**	7.95	8.00	8.05
0.02	0.03	0.04	**21.00**	8.95	9.00	9.05
0.02	0.03	0.04	**22.00**	9.90	9.98	10.05
0.02	0.03	0.03	**23.00**	10.90	11.00	11.10
-	-	0.03	**24.00**	11.90	11.98	12.05
0.01	0.02	0.03	**25.00**	12.90	12.98	13.05
0.01	0.02	0.03	**26.00**	13.80	13.95	14.10

Fig. 6.1 BITO ETF Options chain Expiry Date Oct 21, 2022

So the underlying asset for the options is the ETF with ticker symbol "BITO" and while recording (on September 17, 2022), the last price of the ETF was $12.06. Several strike prices (from $1 to $26) and the corresponding call and put premiums are listed under the "Bid" and "Ask" columns for both of them.

From the options chain above, if a speculator wants to **buy** the $11 "Call" option, she will have to *pay* $1.70 per share as premium (the "Ask" price). In any financial transaction, always two counter-parties need to be involved: the buyer and the seller. Thus if another speculator wants to get involved as an **options seller**, she will *sell* the $11 "Call" option to the buyer and will *receive* $1.61 per share as premium (the "Bid" price).

The "Mid" price is nothing but the **average** of the "Bid" and "Ask" prices. Please also note that, some of the options premium are $0.00 (zero) and represented by "-".

ETF and stock options are always bought and sold under multiple of 100 shares of underlying asset called the "**unit**".

When an options buyer invokes her right to buy or sell the underlying security it's called **"exercising"** [1] the option.

The option notation like: "5 BITO October 21, 2022 $11 Call" provides the buyer the **option** to buy 5 units (=500) of BITO shares at $11 (from the options seller) irrespective of whatever price it reaches on (or before) October 21, 2022 and hence the name "option".

For example, if BITO price stays *over* $11 on October 21, 2022 the call options buyer will exercise her option and the options seller will be **obligated** to sell 500 BITO shares to the buyer at $11 although the market price of BITO was greater than $11 on that day.

However, if BITO price goes *below* $11 on October 21, 2022 the call options buyer will **not** execute her option (the rationale becomes, as the market price of BITO is lower than $11 on that day, there is no point to buy it for $11 from the options seller) and it will expire worthless. In this case, however, the options buyer will lose the premium she'd paid (=$850) to buy the options and the options seller will profit the premium (=$805) she'd received while selling the options. As an aside, as trading is a zero sum game, the difference of premium of $45 will be received by the Market Maker or Specialists [2] who provides liquidity for this option.

In the same token, from the options chain above if a speculator wants to **buy** the $12 "Put" option she will have to *pay* $1.07 as premium (the "Ask" price). If another speculator wants to be the options **seller**, she will *sell* the $12 "Put option" and *receive* $1.05 as premium (the "Bid" price).

Again, the option notation like: "5 BITO October 21, 2022 $12 Put" provides the put options buyer the option to sell 500 BITO shares at $12 (to the options seller) irrespective of whatever price it reaches on (or before) October 21, 2022.

Now, if BITO price stays below $12 on October 21, 2022 the put options buyer will exercise her option and the options seller will be obligated to buy 500 BITO shares from the options buyer at $12 although the market price of BITO was less than $12 on that day.

However, if BITO price goes *above* $12 on October 21, 2022, the put options buyer will **not** execute her option (the rationale becomes, as the market price of BITO is greater than $12 on that day, there is no point to sell it for $12 to the options seller) and it will expire worthless. In this case, however the put options buyer will lose the premium she'd paid (=$535) to buy the options and the options seller will profit the premium (=$525) she'd received for selling the options. The $10 difference in premium will be received by the Market Maker or Specialists as usual for providing liquidity for this option.

From the above discussion it is evident that, the options buyer has the "**right**" to execute the options (to take delivery or provide delivery of the underlying assets) only when felt necessary; however **no** obligation to execute it ever (options will expire worthless in this case).

Options buyer buys this "right" by paying the premium. On the other hand, the options seller relinquishes her right by collecting the premium and becomes **obligated** to take delivery or provide delivery of the underlying assets if and when the options buyer executes her contract(s).

This is the stark difference of options with other form of derivatives like Future contracts [3] in which buyer and seller are **both** obligated to execute their contracts.

Why options prices are also called the "premiums"?

We generally relate premiums with the insurances and please note that, the put option is analogous to insurance.

We as insurance buyers, buy the "right" to receive monetary and/or other form of compensations if and when some unfortunate events occur and to compensate the risk the insurance company takes, we pay the prices to that company called the "risk premiums" or simply premiums. On the other hand, as the insurance company collects the risk premiums, it is **obligated** to provide us compensation if and when some unfortunate events occur.

In case of put options, the seller is analogous to the insurance company. The put option buyer pays the option *price* to the seller to compensate the risk the seller takes (of losing money in overall transactions) and buys the "right" that the seller will be **obligated** to take delivery of the underlying assets if it's price decreases and when the options buyer exercises her contract(s).

Thus the options prices are nothing but the "risk premiums" the buyer pays to the seller and hence also called as options premiums.

Options Pricing Model and Implied Volatility

An option pricing model uses a variety of input parameters to derive the theoretical price of an option. There are several pricing models available and out of them one of the most popular one is the Black–Scholes Model with Merton's extension (or simply the Black-Scholes-Merton model [4]) which we are going to discuss in this book.

According to the Black-Scholes-Merton model, if 'p' is the price or value of an option, it depends upon the following *six* parameters:

x = the price of the underlying asset, c = the strike price, σ = volatility of the underlying asset, r = risk-free interest rate, t = time to expiration and q = dividend yield by the underlying asset.

In "A Brief History of Time" [5] Professor Stephen Hawking mentioned that, "each equation included in the book would halve the sales". After reading that, as I do care that my book sales well, I became much reluctant to use complex formulas in my books.

Thus I mentioned the original formulas by Black, Scholes and Merton in endnotes only for reference and now present the simplest mathematical form of the Black-Scholes-Merton model as below:

p = f(σ , x, c, r, t, q) where "f" represents the Black, Scholes and Merton pricing model.

Please note, in the equation above volatility (σ) is the only **unknown** parameter and the rest are known and readily available as financial data. This volatility is not the historical/statistical volatility of the underlying stock/ETF as by definition historical volatility is the annualized standard deviation (fluctuations) of **past** price movements of stock/ETF and thus backward-looking; however this volatility is typically of more interest to retail option traders, because of it's futuristic nature, thus it is forward-looking.

This volatility is called **implied** volatility as it's what the marketplace is "implying" to be the volatility of the stock/ETF in the future based on the changes in price of an option.

Implied volatility is a dynamic figure that changes based on activity in the options market. When implied volatility increases (decreases), the price of options will increase (decrease) as well, provided all other things remain constant.

How implied volatility is derived?

Based on truth and rumors in the market, options prices begin to change. If there's an earnings announcement, odd events like mergers/acquisitions, rumors of bankruptcy or a major court decision is coming up traders will alter trading patterns on certain options for those stocks/ETFs. That drives the price of those options up or down, independent of stock/ETF price movement. By gauging significant imbalances in supply and demand, implied volatility represents the expected fluctuations of an underlying stock/ETF over a specific time frame.

Please note that, if there is any intrinsic value in the option price it will never change; only the options' time value will be affected. Options' time value will change because of the perceived potential (future) price movements of the stock/ETF. As implied volatility is an estimate or projection of the future volatility it often overstates the expected move of the stock/ETF.

Implied volatility can then be derived from the price of the option. As a matter of fact, if there were no options traded on a given stock/ ETF, there would be no way to calculate the implied volatility.

Assuming that, there exists an inverse function $g = f^{-1}$ we can simply derive implied volatility (σ) from the Black-Scholes-Merton model as below: $\sigma = g(p, x, c, r, t, q)$

Other options nomenclatures

1. Options exercise style: American or European

The style of an option refers to when that option is exercisable. In general, there are two different styles of option exercise: American-style and European-style.

Each American-style option may be exercised at any time prior to its expiration. All Stock and ETF options follow American-style exercise.

A European-style option may be exercised only on its expiration date. Mostly all index options follow European-style exercise.

It's important to note that, in practice, although there are a few exceptions, American-style options are **almost never** exercised prior to expiration; so this distinction tends not to matter much. When the option buyers buy options and the stock/ETF price shoots up (for call options) or goes down (for put options), most buyers would simply sell the option contracts to someone else, not exercise them.

However important *exception* of early exercising of American options may happen if an investor wrote Uncovered (Naked) calls or Covered calls on dividend paying ETF/stocks [6]. Please see the endnotes for details.

2. Options moneyness: Out of The Money (OTM), In The Money (ITM) and Nearest To the Money (NTM)

Options moneyness is the relationship between the price of the underlying asset and the strike prices of the options in an option chain.

A call option is Out of The Money (OTM) when its strike price is **higher** than the price of the underlying asset and a put option is Out of The Money (OTM) when its strike price is **lower** than the price of the underlying asset.

Call options are In The Money (ITM) when its strike price is **lower** than the price of the underlying asset and put options are In The Money (ITM) when its strike price is **higher** than the price of the underlying asset.

In Figure 6.1 above, for BITO options chain, the OTM strikes are **shaded** for call and put options and the non-shaded strikes denote ITM for call and put options.

Nearest To the Money (NTM) strike is defined as the strike price which is **nearest** to the market price of the underlying asset. In figure 6.2 below, the market or spot price of QQQ was $57.52 and so the nearest strike price became $58.00.

Please also note that based on the market price of QQQ (=$57.20), the strike price of $58 is slightly OTM for the call and slightly ITM for the put option.

Calls						Strike ▼	Puts					
Last	Chg	Bid	Ask	Vol	OpInt		Last	Chg	Bid	Ask	Vol	OpInt
	Jul11 Calls					QQQ @ 57.52	Spot Price					
4.50	0	4.50	4.69	00	7,401	53.00	0.01	0	0.01	0.02	00	61,745
3.56	0	3.56	3.67	00	34,316	54.00	0.03	0	0.02	0.03	00	71,423
2.59	0	2.61	Nearest The Money Options				0.05	0	0.05	0.06	00	116,339
1.65	0	1.67	1.73	00	38,956	56.00	0.12	0	0.11	0.13	00	51,524
0.86	0	0.86	0.90	00	47,449	57.00	0.32	0	0.28	0.30	00	75,332
0.29	0	0.29	0.30	00	56,577	58.00	0.70	0	0.69	0.72	00	85,128
0.06	0	0.05	0.07	00	53,208	59.00	1.45	0	1.45	1.47	00	49,769
0.01	0	0.01	0.02	00	33,922	60.00	2.47	0	2.36	2.45	00	8,078
0.01	0	0	0.01	00	21,073	61.00	2.98	0	3.34	3.53	00	6,444
0.01	0	0	0.01	00	17,773	62.00	4.25	0	4.36	4.51	00	5,483

Fig. 6.2 Options Moneyness: Nearest To the Money (NTM)
Source: OptionTradingPedia.com

Note: In some texts on options moneyness, instead of Nearest To the Money (NTM), the term At The Money (ATM) is used. At The Money (ATM) strike price is defined as the strike price which is **equal** to the market price of the underlying asset.

In options, strike prices are generally defined in 0.50 cents or whole dollar increments (like strike price = 3.50, 112.00 etc.) but in real life, the underlying asset **rarely** closes in 0.50 cents or whole dollar. That's why we use Nearest To the Money (NTM) strike price, as it is a better representative of moneyness in real world.

3. Intrinsic (or Real) and Time (or Extrinsic) values of an option:

Theoretical price of an option (for a given expiry month) depends upon two factors viz. Intrinsic (or Real) Value plus the Time (or Extrinsic) Value of the option.

Thus the time value of an option can be defined as:

Time value = option price – intrinsic value   **[Equation 6.1]**

Intrinsic Value:

Intrinsic value of an option measures how much the option is in-the-money (ITM). Thus only the ITM options can have intrinsic values and time values both; however the OTM options have **no** intrinsic values and only the time values.

Based on the discussion above, the intrinsic value of an option can be defined as:

Intrinsic Value of an ITM Call = Spot (live) price of the underlying asset – Strike price of the ITM Call.

Intrinsic Value of an ITM Put = Strike price of the ITM Put – Spot (live) price of the underlying asset.

Example of intrinsic value:

From Figure 6.2 above, intrinsic value of the ITM call, "QQQ, July 15, 2011 $57 Call" = $57.52 -$57=$0.52.

As a different example, the OTM put, "QQQ, July 15, 2011 $57 Put" option would have an intrinsic value of zero ($57-$57.52 = -$0.52) because the intrinsic value cannot be negative.

Similarly, intrinsic value of the ITM put, "QQQ, July 15, 2011 $60 Put" = $60-$57.52= $2.48.

As a different example, the OTM call, "QQQ, July 15, 2011 $60 Call" would have an intrinsic value of zero ($57.52- $60 = -$2.48) because the intrinsic value cannot be negative.

Time Value:

As discussed earlier, the option sellers are **obligated** to take the "risk" of being exposed in the market till the expiry of the option. So, they must be compensated through premiums for taking this risk. This risk premium (or simply premium) is also called the time premium as it's based on the time left for the option.

Thus the time value of an OTM option is defined as the premium of the option corresponding to the time left to maturity of the option.

Please note that, this premium depends upon the volatility (discussed later) of the underlying asset as well.

Example of time value:

Based on the Equation 6.1 above, Time value = option price – intrinsic value

Now from Figure 8.2 above, the option price of the ITM call, "QQQ, July 15, 2011 $57 Call" will be ($0.86+$0.90)/2 = $0.88 [**Note:** As there is always a spread between the bid and ask prices, we typically consider the **mid-price** of these two as option price].

Earlier above, we calculated the intrinsic value for this option as $0.52.

So, the time value of "QQQ, July 15, 2011 $57 Call" will be $0.88-$0.52=$0.36.

Similarly, for the OTM put, "QQQ, July 15, 2011 $57 Put" will have the time value as ($0.28+$0.30)/2 = $0.29 as it has zero intrinsic value.

4. Open Interest:

Open interest is the number of options contracts that are held by options traders as active positions. These positions have been opened but have not been closed out or expired. To close out an option, the trader must take an offsetting position (i.e. options buyer has sold or exercised her options position or the options seller has bought back her options position).

Open interest increases once again when options buyers open more new long positions or sellers take on new short positions in an amount greater than the number of contracts that were closed that day.

Example: Assume that the open interest of the IBM $200 May 19, 2023 Call option is 0. The next day an options trader buys 20 of this call as a new position. Open interest for this particular call option is now 20. The day after, five contracts were closed, 10 were opened thus the open interest increased by five to 25.

5. Some important financial measures (aka "Greeks") of an option:

Financial measures of an option define the sensitivity of option prices to its underlying variables such as the price or volatility of the underlying asset. In colloquial, these financial measures are called the "Greeks" as they are (mostly) denoted by Greek alphabets.

a) Theta (θ): As option is a "wasting" or decaying asset, the option price (i.e. premium) loses value over the passage of time. This means as time moves closer to the maturity of an option, the option premium loses its' **time value** as long as everything else is constant.

Thus if an option was ITM, at option expiration, only the intrinsic value of that option remains and for an OTM option the value left is nothing.

The measure of theta quantifies the time decay or the erosion of the value of an option as time passes. Because theta represents the risk of time value to the option buyer, it is always expressed as a negative number to the long options (call and put both).

Essentially, theta is the first derivative of the price of the option with respect to the time (towards maturity of the option contract). Mathematically speaking:

$$\theta = -\frac{\partial V}{\partial T}$$

∂ denotes the first derivative and V is the price of the option and T denotes the time towards maturity.

Conversely, time decay is favorable to the options seller. Options seller benefits from time decay as the value of the options become less as the time to expiration approaches. Consequently, it is cheaper for options seller to buy back the options to close out the short positions.

Example: An option buyer purchases a call option for SPY ETF with a strike price of $150 for $4. The underlying ETF is trading at $155. The option has five (5) days until expiration and the theta is $1. Thus, the value of the option will drop $1 per day until it reaches the expiration date.

Assume the underlying ETF remains at $155 and three (3) days have passed. The option value will be worth approximately $1. This is unfavorable to the option buyer as, if she wants to close out this option now she will incur a loss of $3 per ETF although everything else is unchanged besides the time.

Now look at the same set of transactions to the option seller's perspective. First she'd sold the option to the buyer for $4. Now after three (3) days when the buyer is selling back the option (to close out), the seller is buying it back making $3 profit per ETF. So, the theta is becoming favorable to the options seller as everything else is unchanged besides the time in this case.

b) Delta (Δ): Delta *measures how much the price of* an option is expected to move based on every $1 change in underlying security.

Essentially, delta is the first derivative of the price of the option with respect to the price of the underlying security. Mathematically:

$$\Delta= \frac{\partial V}{\partial S}$$

∂ denotes the first derivative and V is the price of the option and S is the price of the underlying. Delta measures the "speed" at which the option price will change with respect to a move in the underlying asset.

Long stocks/ETFs always have a delta of 1 and short stocks/ETFs always have a delta of -1.

Calls always have positive delta between 0 and 1 and puts always have negative delta, between 0 and -1.

The At-The-Money (ATM) (i.e. where stock price = strike price) call always have delta = 0.50 and the ATM put always have delta = -0.50.

Example: If a call has a delta of 0.40 and the underlying stock/ETF goes up $1, in theory, the price of the call will also go up about $0.40. If the stock/ETF goes down $1, in theory, the price of the call will also go down about $0.40.

Also if a put has a delta of -0.55 and the stock/ETF goes up $1, in theory, the price of the put will go down $0.55. If the stock/ETF goes down $1, in theory, the price of the put will go up $0.55.

c) Vega (ᴠ): Vega is not a Greek letter; however has been coined by traders and is denoted by the Greek letter Nu (ν).

Vega measures, the sensitivity or rate of change of the option price with respect to the **implied volatility** of the underlying asset. If the volatility of the underlying asset increases by 1%, Vega measures how much the option price will change based on that.

Essentially, Vega is the first derivative of the option price with respect to the volatility of the underlying asset. Mathematically:

$$\nu = \frac{\partial V}{\partial \sigma}$$

∂ denotes the first derivative and V is the price of the option and σ is the implied volatility of the underlying asset.

Example: Assume QQQ is trading at $50 per share in January and a February $52.50 call option has a bid price of $1.50 and an ask price of $1.55. Assume that the Vega of the option is 0.25 and the implied volatility is 30%.

If the implied volatility increases to 31%, then the option's bid and ask price should increase to $1.75 and $1.80, respectively ($0.25 added to bid and ask prices).

However, if the implied volatility is decreased to 27%, the bid and ask price should theoretically drop to $1.00 and $1.05 respectively.

d) Gamma (Γ): Gamma measures the rate of change of option Delta based on every dollar move of the underlying stock/ETF. As delta is a first derivative of the price of an option, gamma is a second derivative.

Gamma measures the "speed" at which an option's delta will change with respect to a move in the underlying asset. Thus Gamma can be considered a measure of option price "acceleration" with respect to a move in underlying asset.

Mathematically, gamma is the convexity of the delta as Gamma measures the curvature of option delta and can be represented as:

$$\Gamma_c = \frac{\partial^2 C}{\partial S^2} = \frac{\partial \Delta_c}{\partial S}$$

$$\Gamma_p = \frac{\partial^2 P}{\partial S^2} = \frac{\partial \Delta_p}{\partial S}$$

∂ denotes the first derivative, S is the price of the underlying, C/P is the price of the call/put option, and Δ is the delta of the option (call or put).

Example: Suppose QQQ ETF is trading at $50.12 and its $50 Call option has a delta of 0.5 and a gamma of 0.10. Then, for every $1 move in the ETF price, the delta will be adjusted by a corresponding 0.10. This means, a $1.00 increase of QQQ will mean that the option's delta will increase to 0.60. Likewise, a $2.00 decrease in price of the ETF will result in a corresponding decline in delta to 0.30.

Important Note: For all practical purposes, readers will **not** have to calculate these Greeks or option prices or implied volatilities. Every options trading platform readily provides such information and more.

However, these are the bare minimum theoretical discussion we need to undergo before we proceed to the options strategies.

Effect of "Greeks" over Call and Put options:

As we discussed above, the Greeks are important measures in understanding different elements of risk in trading options. The Greeks are constantly changing and do not works in isolation, meaning that movement in one Greek would likely to affect others. Below I provide a framework which depicts the Effect of "Greeks" over Call and Put options both long and short:

Greeks Long/Short	Delta	Vega	Theta	Gamma
Long call	+	+	-	+
Long put	-	+	-	+
Short call	-	-	+	-
Short put	+	-	+	-

Fig. 6.3 Effect of "Greeks" over Call and Put options
Courtesy: blog.lyra.finance/the-option-greeks

A plus sign means that an increase in this measure will work in options favor, whereas a minus sign means that this measure is unfavorable for the options position. For example, delta is positive for long call means the position will gain value for an increase in stock/ETF price or a short put option has a positive theta means that the time works favorably for this option position.

Endnotes

[1] Exercise of an option: When an investor *exercises* an *option*, she buys (in case of call option) or sells (in case of put option) the security at a particular price as specified in the *option* contract. If that was an American style option, that could be exercised any time before the expiration of the option; however if it was a European style option, it could be exercised only at the expiration of the option.

[2] Market makers and specialists: Market makers are major brokers and/or dealers who are the members of a major stock exchange (like NASDAQ) and whose role is to increase liquidity of securities in that exchange and maintain a fair and orderly market. These market makers maintain inventories of securities and buy and sell those from their own accounts to individual customers and other dealers. Each market maker on NASDAQ is required to give a two-sided quote, meaning they must state a firm bid and ask price that they are willing to honor. Once an order is received from a buyer, the market maker immediately sells off their position of shares from their own inventory to complete the order. Similarly, once an order is received from a seller, the market maker immediately buys those securities to complete the order. Market makers are openly competitive (as evident in tight spreads) and as a result, traders generally get the best price.

A specialist is a person or business entity who is a member of the New York Stock Exchange and whose role is to facilitate trading in certain stocks. Specialists must make a market in those stocks by displaying their best bid and ask prices during trading hours. They also are required to maintain a "fair and orderly market" in the stocks they trade. They do this by stepping in with their own capital to help reduce market volatility when there are not sufficient buyers or sellers. The rules of the exchange prohibit specialists from trading ahead of investors who have placed orders to buy or sell a security at the same price.

From the discussions above in fact, a specialist is a market maker. The term "specialist" is generally associated with stocks and is somewhat dated.

[3] Future Contract: A future contract is a legally binding agreement to buy or sell a standardized asset on a specific date. Futures contracts are "standardized," or effectively interchangeable, and spell out certain specifications, including:

- Quality and quantity of a commodity
- Unit pricing of the asset and minimum price fluctuation (tick size)
- Date and geographic location for physical "delivery" of the underlying asset (but actual delivery rarely happens because most contracts are liquidated before the delivery date)

For example, a December 2023 corn futures contract traded on the CME Group represents 5,000 bushels of the grain to be delivered by a certain date in December 2023.

Please note that, in future contracts buyer and seller both are obligated to execute their contracts (unless liquidated the contracts before expiration); however in case of options, buyers are **never** obligated to execute the contracts (thus the "buyer" has option to execute the contract or not and hence the name "option").

[4] Black-Scholes-Merton model: is a mathematical model for the dynamics of a financial market containing options. From the partial differential equation in the model, known as the Black–Scholes equation, one can deduce the Black–Scholes formula, which gives a theoretical estimate of the call and put prices of European-style options. Fischer Black and Myron Scholes published the equation and the model in 1973 in an article titled "The Pricing of Options and Corporate Liabilities", in the *Journal of Political Economy.* Robert C. Merton was the first to publish a paper expanding the mathematical understanding of the options pricing model, and coined the term "Black–Scholes options pricing model". Merton and Scholes received the 1997 Nobel Memorial Prize in Economic Sciences for their work. Although ineligible for the prize because of his death in 1995, Black was mentioned as a contributor by the Nobel Academy.

The Black-Scholes-Merton equation can be described as a second order parabolic partial differential equation:

$$\frac{\partial V}{\partial t} + \frac{1}{2}\sigma^2 S^s \frac{\partial^2 V}{\partial S^2} + rS\frac{\partial V}{\partial S} - rV = 0$$

The equation describes the price of security options over time.

Pricing a Call Option

The price of a call option C is given by the following formula:

$$C(S_t, t) = N(d_1)S_t - N(d_2)PV(K)$$

Where:

- $d_1 = \frac{1}{\sigma\sqrt{T-t}}\left[\log\left(\frac{S_t}{K}\right) + \left(r + \frac{\sigma^2}{2}\right)(T - t)\right]$
- $d_2 = d_1 - \sigma\sqrt{T - t}$
- $PV(K) = Ke^{-r(T-t)}$

Pricing a Put Option

The price of a put option P is given by the following formula:

$$P(S_t, t) = Ke^{-r(T-t)} - S_t + C(S_t, t) = N(-d_2)Ke^{-r(T-t)} - N(-d_1)S_t$$

Where:

- **N** – Cumulative distribution functions of the standard normal distribution. It represents a standard normal distribution with mean = 0 and standard deviation = 1
- **T-t** – Time to maturity (in years)
- **S_t** – Spot price of the underlying asset
- **K** – Strike price
- **r** – Risk-free rate
- **σ** – Volatility of returns of the underlying asset

Assumptions of the Black-Scholes-Merton (BSM) Model

- **Lognormal distribution**: The BSM model assumes that stock prices follow a lognormal distribution based on the principle that asset prices cannot take a negative value; they are bounded by zero.
- **No dividends**: The model assumes that the stocks do not pay any dividends or returns.
- **Expiration date**: The BSM model assumes that the options can only be exercised on its expiration or maturity date. Hence, it does not accurately price American options. It is extensively used in the European options market.
- **Frictionless market**: No transaction costs, including commission and brokerage, is assumed in the model.
- **Risk-free interest rate**: The interest rates are assumed to be constant, hence making the underlying asset a risk-free one.
- **Normal distribution**: Stock returns are normally distributed. It implies that the volatility of the market is constant over time.

- **No arbitrage**: It avoids the opportunity of making a riskless profit in the form of arbitrage.

Limitations of the Black-Scholes-Merton Model

- **Limited to the European market**: As mentioned earlier, the Black-Scholes-Merton model is an accurate determinant of European option prices. It does not accurately value stock options in the US. It is because it assumes that options can only be exercised on its expiration/maturity date.
- **Risk-free interest rates**: The BSM model assumes constant interest rates, but it is hardly ever the reality.
- **Assumption of a frictionless market**: Trading generally comes with transaction costs such as brokerage fees, commission, etc. However, the Black Scholes Merton model assumes a frictionless market, which means that there are no transaction costs. It is hardly ever the reality in the trading market.
- **No returns**: The BSM model assumes that there are no returns associated with the stock options. There is no dividend; however, it is not the case in the actual trading market.

[5] *A Brief History of Time: From the Big Bang to Black Holes*: is a book on cosmology (the study of the Universe) by British physicist Stephen Hawking. It was first published in 1988 by Bantam Publishing. Hawking wrote the book for non-specialist readers with no prior knowledge of scientific theories on astronomy, general relativity and quantum mechanics. In this book he described in non-technical terms about the origin, structure, development and eventual fate of the Universe, which is an object of study in modern physics..

[6] *Covered Call or Uncovered (Naked) Call writing on Dividend paying ETF/Stocks (and early exercise of American options):* Let us discuss first about covered call on dividend paying ETF/stocks and the early exercise of American options on them before we discuss about the uncovered (or naked) call writing.

What is a Covered Call?

A covered call involves selling call option(s) on ETF/stocks that you already own. By owning the stocks, you're "covered" (i.e. protected) if the stock price rises and the call option expires In-The-Money as you don't have to buy the stock from the open market at a higher price.

Example: Say, you already have 1,000 shares of ABC (AmerisourceBergen Corporation) stock which was bought at $72 per share. Now the price of the stock is $73. You sold 10 ABC August 18, 2022 $75 calls for @ $2.00 receiving $2,000 as premium (excluding commissions).

Now, during expiry if the price of the stock becomes $78 (i.e. greater than the strike price of $75), the call options will expire In-The-Money and you will profit $5,000 (excluding commissions) from the covered calls as below:

Profit from premium = $2,000 + profit from stocks = $3 (sold for $75 - bought for $72) * 1,000 shares = $3,000.

Figure 6E.1 below represents the Covered Call diagram of the example above.

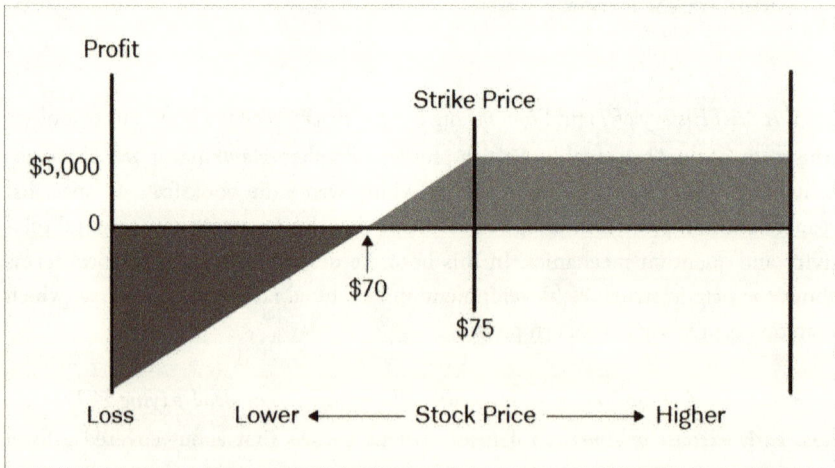

Fig. 6E. 1 Covered call diagram for ABC (AmerisourceBergen Corporation) stock

Please note that, as the call options seller have the obligations to deliver the stocks to the buyer, you are "covered" against this obligation as you already have the ABC stocks (for which you paid only $72/share) and didn't have to buy the stocks from the open market in a higher price of $78/share to fulfill the obligation during options expiration and hence the name.

Please also note that, the covered calls create some immediate downside protection because you wouldn't experience a loss on the position unless the stock you bought for $72 a share dropped below $70 (=$72 buy price -$2.00 commission received), i.e. the breakeven price. That even if the stock price dropped to zero (stock price cannot be negative), you would still have $2,000 from the 10 covered calls you sold.

Normally, selling a call option is associated with a risk that, it exposes the seller to losses if the stock soars below the breakeven price. In the example above, if ABC stock soars below $70, the covered call writer will incur a loss. However, by owning the underlying stock, you limit those potential losses and can generate income.

Another associated risk with the covered call strategy is the opportunity risk of not participating in a large stock price rise. The covered call writer does not fully participate in a stock price rise above the (strike price plus the premium received.)

In the example above, during expiry as the ABC stock rose to $78, her profit is limited to the basis of $77 only. If the investor sold the stocks directly at $78 without writing the covered call, her profit should have been $6,000. So, in the event of a substantial stock price rise, covered call writers are subjected to opportunity loss.

Thus Covered call strategy should be employed by investors if she feels the market id slightly bullish or simply range-bound.

In conclusion, a covered call is a options hedging strategy, in which investor sells some of the stock's upside for a period of time in exchange for the option premium.

What is a Uncovered (or Naked) Call selling?

Simply put, Uncovered or naked call selling or writing is an options strategy where the investor sell the calls without owning the associated stocks before hand.

In the example above, if the investor did **not** own any share of ABC (AmerisourceBergen Corporation), however sold 10 ABC August 18, 2022 $75 calls for @ $2.00 premium will be the example of uncovered or naked call writing. The maximum profit in case of naked call selling is only the premium received and which is $2,000 in this case.

Like covered call selling a naked call option is also associated with the risk that, it exposes the seller to losses if the stock soars below the breakeven price however the breakeven price for naked call is always higher than the breakeven price for the covered call.

In this case if ABC stock soars below the breakeven price of $73 (=$75 strike price - $2 premium received), the naked call writer will incur a loss. This is a stark difference with respect to covered call writing in which the breakeven price is much lower (=$70).

Figure 6E.2 below represents the Uncovered (or naked) Call sell diagram:

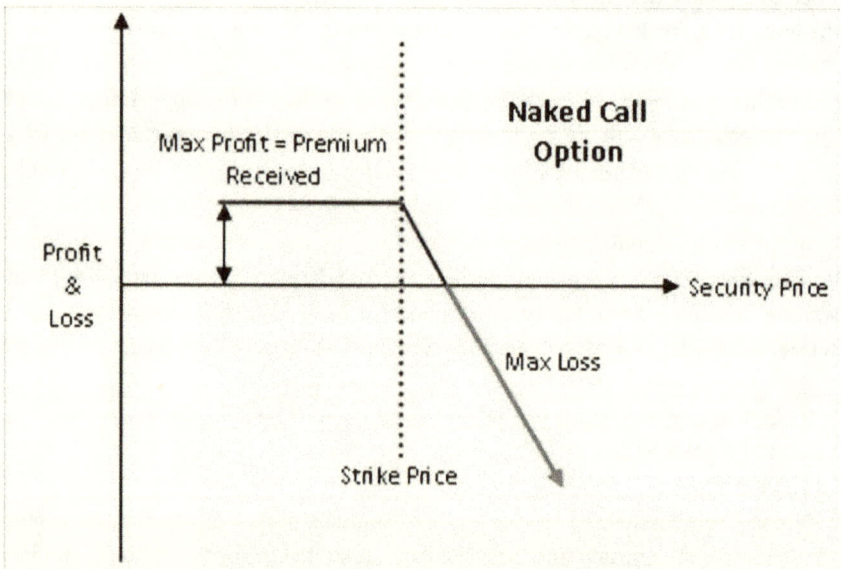

Figure 6E.2 Diagram on Uncovered (Naked) Call Selling

Now in the event that the stock price has dropped to zero, the naked call writer will still have $2,000 from the premium she has received as similar to the covered call writing.

However, the biggest risk in naked call selling is that, if the stock price rises substantially (in theory the stock price can go to the infinite), the seller will experience a huge loss in her trade. For example, if before expiry of the options, great news come for the stock ABC (AmerisourceBergen Corporation) and the stock skyrockets to $200, the naked options seller will lose $198 per stock or whopping $198,000 in total! However, the covered call writer in the above example will still profit $5,000 in this case.

Please also note that, the opportunity loss for the covered call seller is also a whopping $123,000 (=($200-$72-$3-$2)*1,000) in this case.

The effect of dividend and early exercise of American style Options

If for some reason, an (American Style) option is exercised early, the buyer will have to pay the remaining time value of the respective option. For example, if an option expires sixty days from now and a buyer wants to exercise it today, she will have to pay back the time value of these remaining sixty days for that option. This is an inescapable trade-off and inner mechanism of an option.

As an In-The-Money (ITM) option consists mostly the intrinsic value, the time value of an ITM option is low in general. Also, if the expiry date is very nearby (one or two weeks from now), the time value becomes negligible in case of an ITM option.

Going back to the example above... the upcoming Ex-dividend date for ABC (AmerisourceBergen Corporation) stock is August 12, 2022 and it will pay $0.46 dividend. In the example above, the sold calls of $75 strike price will expire on August 18, 2022 and it's an American Style options.

Now if on August 11, 2022 (one day before the ex-dividend date) the stock price stays above the strike price of $75, there is a huge possibility that this call will be exercised early on this date by the options buyers. That's because, if an investor buys the stock on or after the ex-dividend date, the investor does not receive the dividend and hence the name. So, an investor must own the stock *before* the ex-dividend date. Whoever owns the stock as of the ex-dividend date receives the cash dividend, so owners of call options might choose to exercise certain ITM options early to capture the cash dividend.

As long as the stock price is above the strike price, the options is In-The-Money (ITM) and as we discussed above the time value for an ITM option is very low in general. Also if the call options are exercised on August 11, 2022, it's only eight (8) days before the expiry of this option, so we can consider the time value of these ITM options is actually negligible .

Since options holders are not entitled to either regular or special dividends paid by the underlying stocks/ETF, this will enable the investor to capture that dividend. It should more than offset the marginal time value lost due to an early exercise.

In conclusion, covered call and naked call writers are particularly at risk one day before the ex-dividend date of a dividend paying stock/ETF if certain strikes are In-The-Money (ITM) and the expiry date is very nearby (one or two weeks from now) for those options.

Seven

Tools of the trade - Part I: Two Technical Indicators

> *"It's difficult to make predictions, especially with regards to the future."* – Old Proverb

In chapter IX we will discuss about the core strategy of this book. This strategy uses two technical indicators viz. Keltner Channel and Stochastic Oscillator. Let us discuss about these two indicators first, so that it will help us understand the core strategy better as and when we discuss later:

Keltner Channel

The Keltner channel was originally developed by Chester Keltner, a grain trader, in his 1960 book "How to Make Money in Commodities". Linda Raschke, a successful commodity trader, had re-introduced it with modification in the 1980s. In her modification, the bands are based on the Average True Range (ATR) [1] and which is calculated over 10 periods. This ATR value is then multiplied with a multiplier and added to a 20 period exponential moving average (EMA) [2] for the upper band and subtracted from it for the lower band.

The multiplier value is generally chosen as 2, 2.5 or 3 (in case of extremely volatile financial instruments). If we choose the multiplier as 2.5 it contains 95% of the price action and for all practical purpose of trading that should be sufficient.

So, the middle line in Keltner Channel is an Exponential Moving Average (EMA) and the two outer bands are based on Average True Range (ATR). Because the channel is derived from the ATR, which is a volatility indicator itself, the Keltner channel also *contracts* and *expands* with volatility.

Mathematically, Keltner bands are defined as:

Keltner Middle Line = EMA(20).

Upper Keltner Band = Keltner Middle Line + m*ATR(10) where 'm' is a multiplier and m = 2, 2.5 or 3.

Lower Keltner Band = Keltner Middle Line - m*ATR(10) where 'm' is a multiplier and m = 2, 2.5 or 3.

The recommended use of the Keltner channel is as a filter to signal "runaway" market conditions. Runaway market condition denotes a very strong up or down trend with no or very shallow retracements. When prices close above the upper band, it indicates a breakout in upward volatility. Conversely, when prices close below the lower band, it indicates a sign of weakness and the price will move lower further.

Also another important point to note that, the EMA(20) provides dynamic support/resistance for the price action.

Thus, as the price action breaks above or below the top or bottom channel, a continuation is favored over a retracement back to the opposite channel as below:

- If the price action **breaks above** the band, the trader should consider initiating long positions while liquidating short positions.
- If the price action **breaks below** the band, the trader should consider initiating short positions while exiting long positions.

Let's look at the examples below.

Figure 7.1 a): Buying using Keltner channels on a USD/Swiss Franc (CHF) Forex four hours (H4) chart

Figure 7.1 b): Selling using Keltner channels on a USD/Swiss Franc (CHF) Forex four hours (H4) chart

As the price action breaks above the upper Keltner channel, it signals the runaway uptrend condition and to initiate long positions. Also, as the price action breaks below the lower Keltner channel, it signals the runaway downtrend condition and to initiate short positions. The market should not be traded in counter trade manner in these cases and traders should trail with 2-bar trailing stop [3].

In example 7.1 a) above:

- The trader can initiate a **buy** position at the close of the huge bullish bar which closes above the upper Keltner Channel on Dec 18 for 0.8935.
- Using 2-bar trailing stop, the trader will exit at 0.8985, taking 500 pips [4] profit in one day.

In example 7.1 b) above:

- The trader can initiate a **sell** position at the close of the huge bearish bar which closes below the lower Keltner Channel on Jan 22 for 0.9040.
- Using 2-bar trailing stop, the trader will exit at 0.8950, taking 900 pips profit in two days.

Stochastic Oscillator

The Stochastic Oscillator is a momentum indicator that shows the location of the close relative to the price range (i.e. high-low) over a given number of periods. It was developed by George Lane, a commodity floor broker, in the 1950s.

George Lane, in an article for Technical Analysis of Stocks & Commodities called "Lane's Stochastics," wrote of his indicator (in 1983): This method is based on the observation that as price decreases, the daily closes tend to accumulate ever closer to their extreme lows of the daily range. Conversely, as prices increase, the daily closes tend to accumulate ever closer to the extreme highs of the daily range.

Stochastics is a momentum indicator meant to give traders a feel for when the market might be getting ready to change direction. According to an interview with Lane in Trader Profiles magazine, the Stochastic Oscillator "doesn't follow price, it doesn't follow volume or anything like that. It follows the speed or the momentum of price. As a rule, the momentum changes direction before price." "The slowdown of momentum happens before the change of direction," continued Lane... "It's a leading indicator to the change in direction. That's what Stochastics does. It predicts the direction of movement." As such, bullish and bearish divergences in the Stochastic Oscillator can be used to foreshadow reversals. This was the first, and most important, signal that Lane identified.

As the Stochastic Oscillator is range-bound (values between 0 and 100), it is also useful for identifying overbought and oversold levels. A Stochastic reading of 80 indicates a market that is overbought while a reading of 20 indicates a market that is oversold.

The stochastic oscillator consists of two lines called a %D line and a %K line. The %K line—also known as the "raw" stochastic—is derived by determining the ratio between the current session's close less the lowest point for a specific number of period and the highest point for a specific number of period less the lowest point for that specific number of periods. This ratio is multiplied by 100 to arrive at a value for %K.

So mathematically, %K = (current close – lowest low)*100 / (highest high – lowest low).

The %D line, also known as the slow line is a moving average of the %K line.

For all practical purpose, we will use %K=7 (with smoothing = 4) and %D=16 in this book.

David Nassar said of the stochastic in his DVD named "Foundational Analysis": "stochastics measure the shifting control of the emotional range (from fear to greed and vice-versa)." Keep this in mind, as we will look into our strategy to exploit the shifting in psychology through stochastic when greed and fear overwhelm the market. This shift is handled through stochastic by bull or bear divergences.

Bull / bear divergences in stochastic oscillator

A divergence in the stochastic oscillator occurs when the stochastic diverges from security prices. For example, if a security makes a high and then a higher high, while the stochastic makes a high and then a lower high, the stochastic is said to be diverging from price. This represents a bearish divergence as depicted in example 7.2 a) below:

Figure 7.2 a): Bearish stochastic divergence for Crude Oil in July 2006 anticipates a sharp correction, sideway trading, a weak bounce and further to the downside.

Similarly, if a security makes a low and then a lower low, while the stochastic makes a low and then a higher low, the stochastic is also diverging from price. This represents a bullish divergence as depicted in example 7.2 b) below:

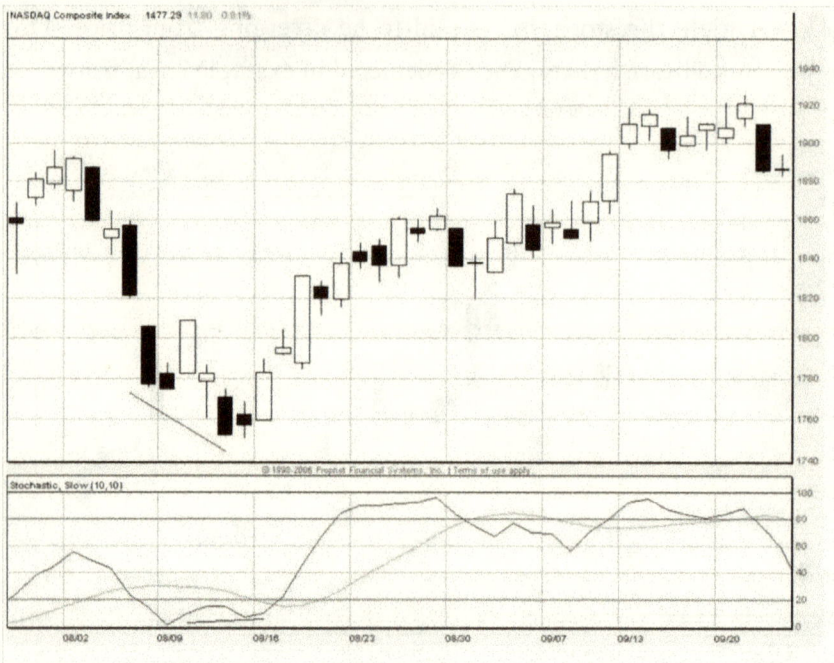

Figure 7.2 b): Bullish stochastic divergence for NASDAQ composite in August 2004.

Divergences occur naturally in strongly trending markets. Recognize that this is a countertrend trade.

Many market gurus recommend against trying to trade tops and bottoms and for good reasons. However, because so much money could be made finding temporary reversals in the market that there will always be the top and bottom seekers. The good news about divergences is that many (if not most) divergences signal traders to go short at market peaks and long at market troughs.

The bad news about divergences is that a trending market will often create multiple divergences before reaching a top or bottom. Traders may find themselves entering positions based on a divergence, only to be stopped out over and over again as the market continues to make higher highs or lower lows.

A tradable divergence has more of a "W" or "M" shape instead of a "stair step" pattern which indicates continued impulse. The move or break from a divergence formation should unfold within a few bars at most. If the market starts to trade sideways for a few bars, the trend is most likely still too strong, and the market can continue on sharply in the direction of the trend.

In order to buy bottoms and sell tops, the trader has to be discriminating in the extreme. If the reversal does not happen and the market moves to form another new low or new high, then the trade must be aborted immediately.

The best trading divergences will come when the price has pushed to the upper or lower Keltner Channel. This indicates that there has been a good price swing and prices may be short-term overextended.

Divergences do not imply an imminent trend reversal, merely a price correction. In a trading range, a retracement back to the 20-period exponential moving average is the initial price objective.

Endnotes

[1] Average True Range (ATR): Average True Range (ATR) is the average of true ranges over a given period. The true range (for today) is defined as the *greatest* of the following:

- Today's high minus today's low,
- The absolute value of (today's high minus yesterday's close) and
- The absolute value of (today's low minus yesterday's close)

Mathematically, Average True Range (ATR) is defined by the following iterative equation:

ATR = (Previous ATR * (n - 1) + TR) / n where n = number of specified periods and TR = True Range.

Please note that, ATR measures volatility taking into account any gaps in the price movement.

[2] Exponential Moving Average (EMA): The Exponential Moving Average is a technical indicator that shows how the price of a security changes over a period of time. The EMA is different from a simple moving average in that it places more weight on recent prices of the security thus the EMA is a type of weighted moving average (WMA) that gives more weight (or importance) to recent price points. Because of its unique calculation, EMA follows price more closely (i.e. more sensitive to price movement) than a corresponding SMA. On one side, it can help identifying trends earlier than an SMA however on the flip side the EMA may experience more short-term changes (whipsaw) than a corresponding SMA.

The aim of all moving averages is to establish the trend or direction in which the price of a security is heading based on past prices. Therefore, all exponential moving averages are lagging indicators as they are not predictive of future prices.

Calculation of EMA

EMA = (K x (C - P)) + P

Where C = Current Price, P = Previous periods EMA (A SMA is used for the first period calculation), K = Exponential smoothing constant = 2/ (selected time period (N) +1)

K, the smoothing constant, applies appropriate weight to the most recent price. It uses the number of periods specified in the moving average.

[3] 2-bar Trailing Stop: In this stop placement strategy, for long trade the stop is placed just below the lowest of two previous bars and for short trade, the stop is placed just above the highest of two previous bars. Thus, for long trade, the trade is automatically exited when price is lower than the previous 2 bars and for short trade, it is automatically exited when price is higher than the previous 2 bars .

[4] Pip: Pip is an acronym for "percentage in point" in Forex. It is the smallest unit, the price could move in a particular currency pair based on Forex market convention.

Most currency pairs are priced out to four decimal places and a single pip will be in the last (fourth) decimal place. Thus it is equivalent to 1/1000 of 0.01%. A pip equals to one basis point.

For example, the smallest units move the USD/CAD currency pair can make is $0.0001 and thus for this currency pair 1 Pip = $0.0001.

This page is intentionally left blank

Eight

Tools of the trade - Part II: Nearest-to-The-Money (NTM) Vertical Debit Spreads

> *"Every morning I get up and look through the Forbes list of the richest people in America. If I'm not there, I go to work."* – Robert Orben

In chapter IX we will discuss about the core strategy of this book. This strategy uses Nearest-to-The-Money (NTM) vertical call spread if we believe that the market is heading towards bullish direction in immediate future and ATM vertical put spread if we believe that the market is heading towards bearish direction in immediate future. Let us discuss about these two spreads first and so that it will help us understand the core strategy better as we discuss later:

What is a vertical spread in options trading?

A vertical spread involves simultaneous buying and selling of options of same no. of contracts, of the same type (i.e. either call or put) and of the **same expiry date**, but at **different strike prices**. The term 'vertical' comes from the position of the strike prices as this type of spreads use the same expiry date.

This is in contrast to a **horizontal** or **calendar spread** which involves simultaneous buying and selling of options of same no. of contracts, of the same type (i.e. either call or put) and of **same strike price**, but with **different expiry dates**. The term 'horizontal' comes from the position of the strike prices as this type of spreads use the same strike price. This spread is also called calendar spread as two different expiry dates takes two different positions temporally.

What is a debit spread?

Options spreads involve in simultaneous buying and selling of the same no. of contracts. If the net amount in these transactions results in a debit from the speculator's account then it's called a debit spread otherwise it's a credit spread. Please see example 1 and 2 below for the debit spreads.

Example 1: NTM vertical debit call (or bull) spread

The price of the stock ABC (AmerisourceBergen Corp) is $158.52 on March 30, 2023. An investor who is **bullish** about this stock decides to buy some vertical **call** spreads for July 2023 expiry date. She bought 10 calls of $160 strike for July 2023 expiry for $6.40 and simultaneously sold 10 calls of $165 strike for the same expiry for $4.05. Thus her account should be debited for $2,350 (plus commission). Please note that:

- $160 is Nearest-to-The-Money (NTM) strike as the stock ABC is selling for $158.52.
- It's a vertical spread as bought and sold calls both were written for the same expiry (July 2023).
- As her account was debited for this spread it's also called a debit spread.
- Debit call spread gains value as the underlying security price increases, thus it's also called a bull call spread.

Profit and loss diagram (for vertical debit call spread)

Figure 8.1 represents the profit and loss diagram for vertical call debit spread. The point 'x1' represents the present price of the stock (=$158.52), 'x3' represents the lower strike price of the calls i.e. the price at which the calls were bought (=$160) and 'x2' represents the higher strike price of the calls i.e. the price at which the calls were sold (=$165).

During expiry, if the price of the stock ABC becomes greater than or equal to the strike price $165 (x2), both the bought and sold calls will be in-the-money and the maximum profit should be achieved as $2,650 (=$5,000-$2,350).

Please note that, in case of vertical NTM debit call spread the reward to risk ratio is generally greater than 1 (in this particular example it is $2,650/$2,350=1.13)

Now during expiry, if the price of the stock ABC becomes less than or equal to the strike price $160 (x3), both the bought and sold calls will expire worthless and the maximum loss should be incurred as $2,350. Please note that, in case of debit spread the maximum loss incurred is only the total amount of premium paid for the spread.

The break-even price point (B) for this call spread is defined as the price at which the calls were bought (=$160) + the premium paid per stock. As for 10 calls spread the total premium paid was $2,350, the break-even point 'B' should be $162.35.

So, during expiry if the stock price becomes less than $165 but great than $162.35 some (not maximum) profit should be achieved. Similarly, during expiry if the stock price becomes greater than $160 but less than $162.35 some (not maximum) loss should be incurred.

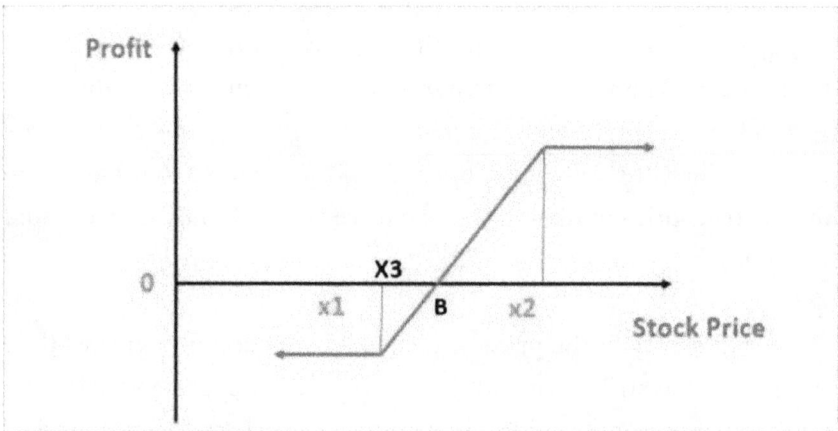

Figure 8.1: Profit and loss diagram for vertical debit call spread

Example 2: NTM vertical debit put (or bear) spread

The price of the stock ABC (AmerisourceBergen Corp) is $158.52 on March 30, 2023. An investor who is **bearish** about this stock decides to buy some vertical **put** spreads for July 2023 expiry date. She bought 10 put of $160 strike for July 2023 expiry for $6.85 and simultaneously sold 10 put of $155 strike for the same expiry for $4.80. Thus her account should be debited for $2,050 (plus commission). Please note that, debit put spread always gains value as the underlying security price decreases, thus it's also called a bear put spread.

Profit and loss diagram (for vertical debit put spread)

Figure 8.2 represents the profit and loss diagram for vertical debit put spread. The point 'P' represents the present price of the stock (=$158.52), 'a' represents the lower strike price of the puts i.e. the price at which the puts were sold (=$155) and 'b' represents the higher strike price of the put i.e. the price at which the puts were bought (=$160).

During expiry, if the price of the stock ABC becomes less than or equal to the strike price $155 (a), both the bought and sold puts will be in-the-money and the maximum profit should be achieved as $2,950 (=$5,000-$2,050).

Please note that, in case of vertical NTM debit put spread the reward to risk ratio is generally greater than 1 (in this particular example it is $2,950/$2,050=1.44)

Now during expiry, if the price of the stock ABC becomes greater than or equal to the strike price $160 (b), both the bought and sold puts will expire worthless and the maximum loss should be incurred as $2,050.

The break-even price point (K) for this put spread is defined as the price at which the puts were bought (=$160) minus the premium paid per stock. As for 10 calls spread the total premium paid was $2,050, the break-even point 'K' should be $157.95.

So, during expiry if the stock price becomes less than $157.95 but great than $155 some (not maximum) profit should be achieved. Similarly, during expiry if the stock price becomes greater than $157.95 but less than $160 some (not maximum) loss should be incurred.

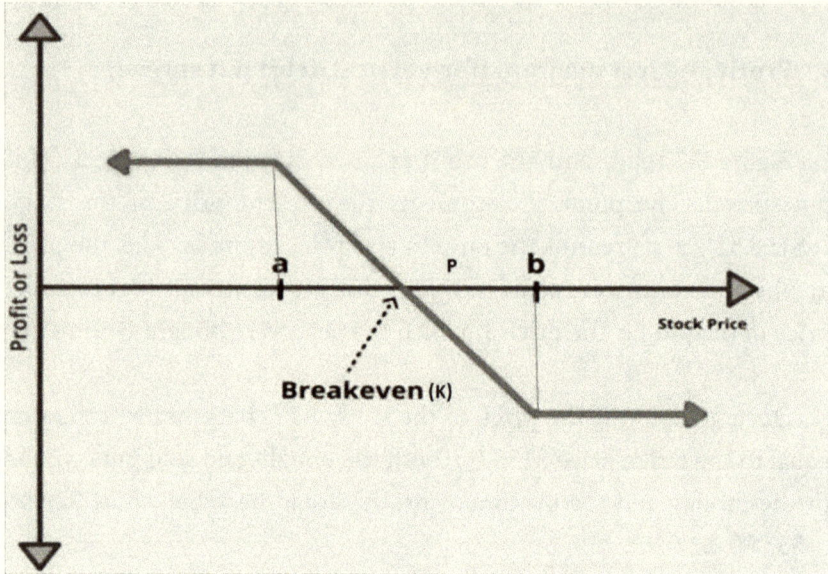

Figure 8.2: Profit and loss diagram for vertical debit put spread

Nine

The Core Strategy

> *"The perfect strategy works every time until you start using it."*-
> Anonymous

The core strategy of this book consists of two parts: the first part deals with the divergences; as we determine the buy (for bullish divergence) or sell (for bearish divergence) price and the price objectives we apply part two of the strategy, which determines how to buy the call spread (for bullish outlook) or put spread (for bearish outlook). Let us discuss two parts of the strategy as below:

Part I of the strategy

1. After the market closes analyze the ETFs (as listed in Chapter V) for their daily charts and look for **divergences**
2. Look for bullish and bearish divergences between the price and the stochastic oscillator (setting %K=7, %D=16 and smoothing = 4).

3. In case of bullish divergence, the oscillator pattern should be a higher low from the previous bottom however the price pattern should still show a lower low from the previous bottom. The oscillator pattern will create a hook like a "V" in this case. This indicates less downside momentum that could foreshadow a bullish reversal.

4. In case of bearish divergence, the oscillator pattern should be a lower high from the previous peak however the price pattern should still show a higher high from the previous peak. This implies less upside momentum that could foreshadow a bearish reversal. The oscillator pattern will create a reverse hook like a "^" in this case.

5. The best price divergences with the oscillator occur when the price move is extended along the Keltner Channels (setting 2.50 times ATR around 20 periods EMA) and we will consider those divergences only.

6. **Buy/Sell Signals:** In case of bullish divergence the trend line of the stochastic oscillator should be directionally up i.e. with positive slope (the present value of the trend line should be greater than it's previous value) -AND- for bearish divergence the trend line of the stochastic oscillator should be directionally down i.e. with negative slope (the present value of the trend line should be less than it's previous value).

7. **Price Objective:** A divergence does not necessarily imply a trend reversal. Thus, we look for a retracement back to the 20-period EMA as the price objective. However, if the divergence has just been established and the price has *already* touched the EMA, we will have to abort the plan to trade. See the examples below.

9.1 Bullish Divergence Strategy Example

Figure 9.1: Bullish Divergence Strategy Example for XBI
Courtesy: Tradingview.com

- See the chart above; in the down pane, Stochastic oscillator is present and with setting %K=7, %D=16 and smoothing = 4. The solid line is the oscillator line and the dotted line is the trend line. The middle line represents median trend value of 50.
- The Keltner Channel setting is 2.50 times ATR around 20 periods EMA. Two solid lines are the channels (upper and lower) and the middle (dotted) line is the 20 periods EMA.
- We see a bullish divergence in XBI; the stochastic oscillator made a higher low B (value 23.70) from the previous bottom A (value 5.82) however the price made a lower low (Y) from the previous bottom (X). These are marked by two lines along the oscillator and the price chart. Thus oscillator is showing less downside momentum that could foreshadow a bullish reversal.
- As the price move was extended along the lower Keltner Channel, we should consider this price divergence and wait for a buy signal
- **Buy signal:** The oscillator created the "V" like hook on August 22, 2023 and the trend line was also directionally up i.e. in positive slope: it's August 22 value was 35.75 which was greater than

the August 21 value of 23.70 (trendline values are not shown in the figure above).

- **Price objective:** The value of the EMA at bar closed on August 22 was $80.07, which has been circled in figure 9.1. Also the closing price for this bar was $78.37, which has been also circled in the figure above.
- **Stop-loss:** The low at the point 'Y' was $75.91 and so we'd placed the stop-loss at $75.90.

We placed the buy limit order for XBI at $78.38 on August 22 overnight and which was filled on August 24. The price objective of $80.07 was achieved on August 31 (after being 5 days in the market) profiting $1.69 per stock (excluding commission).

9.2 Bearish Divergence Strategy Example

Figure 9.2: Bearish Divergence Strategy Example for QQQ
Courtesy: TradingView.com

- We see a bearish divergence in QQQ; the stochastic oscillator made a lower high Y (value 90.06) from the previous top X (value 96.46) however the price made a higher high (B) from the previous top (A). These are marked by two lines along the oscillator and the price chart. Thus oscillator is showing less upside momentum that could foreshadow a bearish reversal.

- As the price move was extended along the upper Keltner Channel, we should consider this price divergence and wait for a sell signal

- **Sell signal:** The oscillator created the "^" (reverse "V") like hook on July 19, 2023, however we *still* had to wait as the trend line was directionally up i.e. in positive slope: on July 24, 2023 (dotted vertical line in the figure above) it went to the negative slope and the sell signal was generated. The July 21 value of the trendline was 56.03 and the July 24 value became 35.96 and so the slope is becoming negative (trendline values are not shown in the figure above).

- **Price objective:** The value of the EMA at bar closed on July 24, 2023 was $372.74, which has been circled in figure 9.2. Also the closing price for this bar was $376.23, which has been also circled in the figure above.

- **Stop-loss:** The high at the point 'B' was $387.98 and so we'd placed the stop-loss at $387.99.

We placed the sell limit order for QQQ at $376.22 on July 24 overnight and which was filled on July 26. The price objective of $372.74 was achieved on August 03 (after being 7 days in the market). We bought back the shares profiting $3.48 per stock (excluding commission).

9.3 Example: When this strategy cannot be used

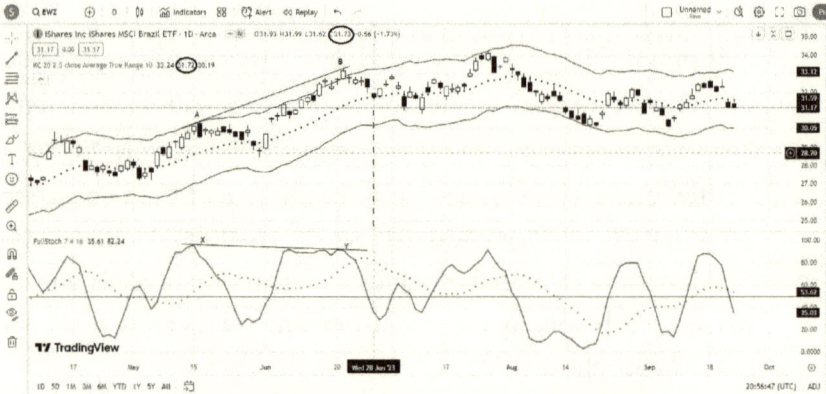

Figure 9.3: Bearish divergence example on EWZ
Courtesy: Tradingview.com

- We see a bearish divergence in EWZ; the stochastic oscillator made a lower high Y (value 91.53) from the previous top X (value 96.06) however the price made a higher high (B) from the previous top (A). These are marked by two lines along the oscillator and the price chart. Thus oscillator is showing less upside momentum that could foreshadow a bearish reversal.

- As the price move was extended along the upper Keltner Channel, We should consider this price divergence and wait for a sell signal

- **Sell signal:** The oscillator created the "^" (reverse "V") like hook on June 22, 2023, however we *still* had to wait as the trend line was directionally up i.e. in positive slope: on June 28, 2023 (dotted vertical line in the figure above) it went to the negative slope and the sell signal was generated. The June 22 value of the trendline was 82.43 and the June 28 value became 80.35 and so the slope is becoming negative (trendline values are not shown in the figure above).

- However, we cannot take the trade as the price has already touched the EMA (EMA = 31.72 and Close = 31.73; both circled in Figure 9.3). Based on point #7 under strategy, a divergence does not necessarily imply a trend reversal. Thus, we look for a retracement back to the 20-period EMA as the price objective. Thus if the divergence has just been established and the price has *already* touched the EMA, we cannot take the trade.

Part II of the strategy

In part one of the strategy, we've determined the buy price (for bullish divergence) or sell price (for bearish divergence) and the respective price objectives.

Divergences are wonderful patterns to use with options. Divergence creates a shift from low volatility to high volatility environment; low volatility environment implies that we can buy options cheap and the high volatility environment implies that we can sell those options in dear prices. Also in options, the leverage is in-built and we can take the advantage of it without taking any external leverage (for example, margin from the broker). So, instead of buying or selling the ETFs/stocks directly, we will **buy** the call spread (for bullish outlook) or put spread (for bearish outlook) **nearest** to the buying / selling price. We will **sell** the call or put spread as our price objective is reached.

In a nutshell, this is the second part of our strategy.

In the next chapter, I will explain why we are buying the call or put spreads instead of buying or shorting the ETFs/stocks directly -OR- buying LEAPS calls or LEAPS puts −OR- buying calls or puts directly. [**Note:** LEAPS has been explained in the next chapter.] Now, the strategy...

1. **Timeframe of the vertical debit spread**: 80-90 days before expiration at the minimum and up to 100-120 days at maximum. (**Rationale**: Below 60 days, there is only effectively 30 days for implied volatility to rise and for Delta and Gamma to move the price before Theta decay accelerates in last 30 days.)

2. **Type of Options**: We will consider monthly options [1] or quarterly options [2] instead of weekly options [3] as the volume and open interests are always greater in monthly or quarterly options than weekly options.

3. **Strike intervals**: Use ETFs/stocks with $1, $2.50 & $5 intervals between strikes. [Note: The ETFs listed in this book all have either $1, $2.5 or $5 interval between strikes] Avoid products with larger strike intervals (e.g. $10) as change in (larger) Delta risk is amplified.

4. **Widen $1 strike interval to $2**: Widening a vertical debit spread to $2 in width allows Delta & Gamma to expand (reasonably) which is required in a directional Debit Spread to gain from the price movement.

5. **Reward to Risk ratio**: Minimum 2:1 i.e. we should pay a maximum of $0.70 premium for a vertical debit spread of $2 interval and so on.

Example vertical debit call spread based on section 9.1

On August 22, 2023 we bought the following **vertical debit call spread** on XBI (closing price = $78.37) after the market closed and it was executed on the next day in open market session:

No. of Contract	Buy/Sell	Strike Price	Expiry Date	Call/Put	Premium	Delta	Theta	Vega	Gamma
10	Buy	78	Nov. 17, 2023	Call	3.05	0.49	-0.746	0.07	0.13
10	Sell	80	Nov. 17, 2023	Call	2.35	0.21	-0.496	0.05	0.10
Net:					0.70	0.28	-0.25	0.02	0.03

Explanation:

- This is a vertical spread as both call contracts (bought and sold) have the same expiry date of November 17, 2023
- The expiry date is about 87 days out
- The (bought) 78 strike price calls are NTM (ATM) as the closing price for XBI ETF was $78.37
- The (sold) 80 strike price calls are OTM
- XBI offers $1 strike interval (78, 79, 80 etc.) however we have widened the strike interval to $2 (78 to 80, skipping the 79 strike) [Please see note 4 above].
- This is a debit spread as we paid $0.70 premium and by definition this is also our maximum risk.
- Also by definition, maximum reward of the spread is the difference between the strike prices minus the premium paid and so the maximum reward/risk ratio becomes about 2:1 = ($2.00-$0.70)/$0.70.
- Debit of the Theta (time decay) for the buy leg is more than the Theta credit received from the sell leg also makes it a (Theta) debit spread as the net Theta is negative.
- Note that, the effect of Vega (volatility) and Gamma are negligible in vertical debit spread as the net values are very low compared to the calls we bought.
- Although debit vertical call starts with net negative Theta, the value of it is much less compared to the calls we bought (-0.25 compared to -0.75). Also, Gamma decreases as the expiry date

comes nearby; the more the Gamma decreases, the Theta increases and becomes net positive Theta near to the expiration.
- The net Delta of 0.28 denotes that if price of XBI increases for $1 the price of the spread will increase for $0.28 and vice-versa.

The closing transactions:

As our target price of $80.07 exceeded on August 31, 2023, we reversed (i.e. closed) this vertical call spread on XBI. Should the value of XBI ever reached below $75.91 (stop-loss point) before August 31, 2023 we should have exited this vertical call spread with a loss.

No. of Contract	Buy/Sell	Strike Price	Expiry Date	Call/Put	Premium
10	Sell	78	Nov. 17, 2023	Call	3.30
10	Buy	80	Nov. 17, 2023	Call	2.25
Net CREDIT:					1.15

So, our net quick five days profit becomes $1.15-$0.70=$0.45 per XBI ETF i.e. $450 in total (excluding commissions) and which was in line of the increase of Delta as above.

Example vertical debit put spread based on section 9.2

July 24, 2023 closing price of QQQ was $376.22 and on July 25, 2023 market open, we bought the following vertical debit put spread:

No. of Contract	Buy/Sell	Strike Price	Expiry Date	Call/Put	Premium	Delta	Theta	Vega	Gamma
10	Buy	376	Oct 20, 2023	Put	6.80	-0.49	-0.712	0.04	0.13
10	Sell	374	Oct 20, 2023	Put	6.24	-0.19	-0.510	0.03	0.09
Net debit on QQQ vertical put spread:					0.56	-0.30	-0.202	0.01	0.04

Explanation:

- The expiry date is about 87 days out
- The (bought) 376 strike price puts are NTM (ATM) as the closing price for QQQ ETF was $376.22
- The (sold) 374 strike price puts are OTM
- QQQ offers $1 strike interval (374, 375, 376 etc.) however we have widened the strike interval to $2 (376 down to 374, skipping the 375 strike) [Please see note 4 above].
- This is a debit spread as we paid $0.56 premium and by definition this is also our maximum risk.
- Also by definition, maximum reward of the spread is the difference between the strike prices minus the premium paid and so the maximum reward/risk ratio becomes about 2.6:1 = ($2.00-$0.56)/$0.56.
- Debit of the Theta (time decay) for the buy leg is more than the Theta credit received from the sell leg also makes it a (Theta) debit spread as the net Theta is negative.
- Note that, the effect of Vega (volatility) and Gamma are negligible in vertical debit spread as the net values are very low compared to the put we bought.
- Although debit vertical put starts with net negative Theta, the value of it is much less compared to the puts we bought (-0.20 compared to -0.71). Also, Gamma decreases as the expiry date

comes nearby; the more the Gamma decreases, the Theta increases and becomes net positive Theta near to the expiration.

• The net Delta of -0.30 indicates that if price of QQQ decreases for $1 the price of the spread will increase for $0.30 and vice-versa.

The closing transactions:

As our target price of $372.74 reached on August 03, 2023, we reversed (i.e. closed) this vertical put spread on QQQ with immediate effect:

No. of Contract	Buy/Sell	Strike Price	Expiry Date	Call/Put	Premium
10	Sell	376	Oct 20, 2023	Put	7.80
10	Buy	374	Oct 20, 2023	Put	6.70
Net CREDIT on QQQ vertical put spread closure:					1.10

So, our net profit becomes $1.10-$0.56=$0.54 per QQQ ETF i.e. $540 in total (excluding commission) in 7 days and which was in line of the decrease of Delta as above.

If things go wrong (i.e. How to adjust the vertical debit spread)

The underlying principle of this chapter is that, we first identify the temporary trend reversal with the help of divergence (between the stochastic and price action) and then apply the debit spread accordingly.

As these trades are reversal trades, we need to be extra careful as the market sentiment may change and in rare cases reversal might *not* actually happen during the life of the debit spread. Like the famous economist John Maynard Keynes *[4]* said, "the markets can remain irrational longer than you can remain solvent."

We've mentioned above that, the life of the debit spreads will be 120 days (max) and we don't recommend going beyond that period as it may unnecessarily increase the Delta and Theta risks; however we can never guarantee that within these 120 days market *will* actually reverse.

In all cases, if the stop-loss point hit for Call or Put vertical debit spread, exit **immediately** by reversing the spread. It will incur loss, however less than the predetermined amount when the position was placed. This is also an adjustment and probably the **best** adjustment in this situation.

Now, we've also mentioned that, we will use ETFs/stocks only with $2.50 & $5 (regular) intervals between strikes and will artificially widen $1 strike interval to $2 by skipping the intermediate strike. Honestly, for the regular $2.50 and $5 intervals we have nothing to adjust and the spread either makes money or loses money. We will have to close the trade if the stop-loss point is hit or near the expiration or profit target is reached. [**Important Note:** You may widen the regular $2.5 strike interval to $5 and it is at your discretion (i.e. risk appetite); however I never recommend to widen the $5 interval to $10 as change in Delta risk (to the larger side) is amplified in this case.]

Now, when $1 strike has been widened to $2 (or $2.5 strike to $5) and you were directionally wrong (you purchased debit Call/Put spread and the market is now going to the opposite direction) but stop-loss was never hit, we can adjust the trade to lower the loss or even breakeven in some cases.

Let's revisit the above examples to show how to adjust the widened $2 strikes the same rule will apply if you ever widened the $2.5 strike to $5 for other ETFs:

- In Example 9.1, if XBI did not reach below $75.91 (stop-loss point) but the price is decreasing, we can adjust the Call debit spread as below. As the price decreased modestly on August 25, 2023 this situation was created and to show the adjustment technique, we bought back the $80 call we sold earlier and sold a new call leg of intermediate strike of $79 (which we skipped earlier). The original call debit spread is shaded in the diagram:

No. of Contract	Buy/Sell	Strike Price	Expiry Date	Call/Put	Premium
10	Buy	80	Nov 17, 2023	Call	1.85
10	Sell	79	Nov 17, 2023	Call	(2.15)
10	Buy	78	Nov 17, 2023	Call	3.05
10	Sell	80	Nov 17, 2023	Call	(2.35)
Net Debit on XBI Vertical Spread Adjustment:					0.40

So, the new structure of the XBI debit call spread will be as below:

XBI New Debit Spread Structure				
No. of Contract	Buy/Sell	Strike Price	Expiry Date	Call/Put
10	Buy	78	Nov 17, 2023	Call
10	Sell	79	Nov 17, 2023	Call

Please remember that, when we are directionally wrong, the sell leg for a debit spread is threatened (as in selling of an option you don't have any right but the obligations to fulfill). Thus, in this case we are buying back the $80 leg which is threatened and selling new calls on intermediate strike of $79 which we skipped earlier.

We have collected some premium in this adjustment and the net debit for this new $1 spread (=$79-$78) is $0.40; which is also the maximum risk in this trade and the Reward to Risk for this adjusted spread becomes, ($1.00-$0.40)/$0.40 = 1.5. By squeezing the call debit spread from $2 to $1 interval, we have also reduced the risk for $0.30 (=$0.70-$0.40) as we were afraid that, the trade may go out of our hand. However, if XBI rebounds we can also make $0.60 (=$1.00-$0.40) per share as a maximum profit in the case later.

Finally, I still believe that, if stop-loss is not triggered, we shall wait without doing adjustment and not being panicked. Often the adjustment could be felt as unnecessary at the end of the trade. Patience gives the market required time to rebound and we should trust the divergence as a very powerful and leading momentum method (indicator) which correctly predicts the upcoming market direction most of the time.

- In Example 9.2, if QQQ did not reach above $387.98 (stop-loss point) but the price is increasing, we can adjust the Put debit spread as below. As the price increased modestly on July 28, 2023 this situation was created and to show the adjustment technique, we bought back the $374 put we sold earlier and sold a new put leg of intermediate strike of $375 (which we skipped earlier). The original put debit spread is shaded here:

No. of Contract	Buy/Sell	Strike Price	Expiry Date	Call/Put	Premium
10	Buy	374	Oct 20, 2023	Put	5.95
10	Sell	375	Oct 20, 2023	Put	(6.15)
10	Buy	376	Oct 20, 2023	Put	6.80
10	Sell	374	Oct 20, 2023	Put	(6.24)
Net Debit on QQQ Vertical Spread Adjustment:					0.36

So, the new structure of the QQQ debit put spread will be as below:

QQQ new Debit Spread Structure				
No. of Contract	Buy/Sell	Strike Price	Expiry Date	Call/Put
10	Sell	375	Oct 20, 2023	Put
10	Buy	376	Oct 20, 2023	Put

We have collected some premium in this adjustment and the net debit for this new $1 spread (=$376-$375) is $0.36; which is also the maximum risk in this trade and the Reward to Risk for this adjusted spread becomes, ($1.00-$0.36)/$0.36 = 1.8. By squeezing the put debit spread from $2 to $1 interval, we have also reduced the risk for $0.20 (=$0.56-$0.36) as we were afraid that, the trade may go out of our hand. However, if QQQ rebounds we can also make $0.64 (=$1.00-$0.36) per share as a maximum profit in the case later.

The other arguments given during the adjustment in example 9.1 above are still valid in this case.

Endnotes

[1] Monthly Options: Monthly options are intermediate term options which expire on the third Friday of each month. So, it has historically 12 monthly expirations. Monthly options are released many weeks before expiration.

[2] Quarterly Options: Quarterly Options are longer term (LEAPS being the longest term options) options which expire on every quarter of the year (March 31, June 30, September 30 and December 31). So, it has historically four expirations in a year. Quarterly options are released many weeks before expiration.

[3] Weekly Options: Weekly Options are short term options which expire every Friday. Weekly options are introduced on Thursdays and expire eight days later on Friday. So, it has historically 52 expirations in a year. While Monthly and Quarterly options generally have excellent liquidity with respect to volume and open interests, for some weekly options there may not be enough liquidity and so the (ask minus bid) spread can be unreasonably big.

[4] John Maynard Keynes: John Maynard Keynes was a renowned British economist who lived from 1883 to 1946. He is best known for his influential contributions to macroeconomics and economic policy. Keynes believed that government intervention was crucial to stabilize the economy during times of recession or depression. His ideas formed the foundation of Keynesian economics, which emphasized the importance of aggregate demand in determining economic output and employment levels. Keynes' theories had a significant impact on economic thought and policy-making, particularly during the Great Depression and post-World War II period. His work continues to shape economic debates and policies to this day.

This page is intentionally left blank

Ten

Why Use Options ATM / NTM Debit Spreads?

> *"We live by the Golden Rules. Those who have the gold make the rules."* - Buzzie Bavasi

Based on the strategy we discussed in the preceding chapter, the following questions may arise; **why ATM/NTM debit spread options have been considered, why don't us:**

1. **Buy or short ETF/stocks directly instead –OR-**
2. **Buy LEAPS puts or LEAPS calls on ETF/stocks instead –OR-**
3. **Buy regular puts or calls on ETF/stocks instead?**

Answer to question #1: Yes, the ETF/stocks can be bought directly however as the inherent leverage is a key feature of options, the buying power amplifies tremendously in options (without taking any margin from the broker), which is absent if the ETF/stocks are bought directly.

Also, in the beginning of the book I've explained the issues with shorting and concluded to play long-only: as we will not short, we will have to forego the bearish divergence opportunities if we have played with the ETF/stocks directly and will play long to be vested in bullish divergence opportunities only.

In example 9.1, by investing only $700 we can control the XBI ETF worth of about $78,000. For example 9.2, by investing only $560 we can control the QQQ ETF worth of $376,000. If we didn't use options, we have had to invest $78,000 for XBI ETF to achieve the same effect and so the buying power has been amplified about 111 times in this case. In example 9.2, if we were dealing directly with QQQ ETF, we'd to forgo the shorting opportunity entirely as we will play long only and won't short. Losing opportunity is a huge disadvantage in this case. However, buying put spread we are mimicking the shorting of QQQ in this case.

Answer to question #2: LEAPS (Long-term Equity AnticiPation Securities) are nothing but longer term options whose expiries are typically 24-36 months from now.

Investors buy call LEAPS with Delta very close to 1 and put LEAPS with Delta very close to -1. Although the capital requirement is less than to purchase the ETF/stocks directly, it is actually very little less. Thus purchasing LEAPS with delta very near to 1 or -1 could be also very expensive and the capital expenditure could be substantial.

In case of example 9.1 if we buy 10 calls of XBI LEAPS of Dec 19, 2025 expiry (which more than 24 months away as of writing) of strike price 40 (it has the highest Delta = 0.91), we need to spend $39 premium per ETF thus investing a total of $39,000. This investment is substantially more than only $700 we need to invest in case of the debit vertical call spread.

Now, in case of example 9.2 if we buy 10 puts of QQQ LEAPS of Dec 19, 2025 expiry for 545 strike price (it has the highest Delta = -0.97), we need to spend $190 premium per ETF thus investing a total of $190,000. This investment is substantially more than only $560 we need to invest in case of the debit vertical put spread.

This boils down to two important questions. The first one becomes: Why an investor will buy call LEAPS with Delta very close to 1 and put LEAPS with Delta very close to -1?

We already know that, Delta is the theoretical estimate of how much an option's value may change given a $1 move up or down in the underlying ETF/Stock. The Delta values range from -1 to +1.

Thus, for the call strike for which the Delta is very close to 1, the premium will increase about $1 if the underlying security moves up for a $1. This is nothing but the mimicking of the security itself and the investor can use *that* call strike as an alternative to ETF/stocks ownership.

In the same token, for the put strike for which the Delta is very close to -1, it will act as a pure shorting of the underlying security and an investor can use it to hedge her current ETF/stock positions.

Now, the second important question. Why LEAPS with Delta close to +1 or -1 is so expensive?

As the expiries of LEAPS are very distant and typically 24-36 months from now, there will be almost NO time values embedded in the premium and it will contain only the intrinsic value of the options. As deep In-The-Money options (Delta closed to +1 or -1) acts like surrogate ETF/Stocks the intrinsic value of the premium will also be very close to the actual value of the ETF/Stocks. So, the leverage characteristic of options is heavily missing in case of deep In-The-Money LEAPS and so they are very expensive in general.

Answer to question #3: Buying regular (expiry between 80-120 days) puts or calls on ETF/stocks is not a great idea as options are depreciating asset and the Theta (time decay) may incur losses even if the ETF/stock price decreases in case of put or ETF/stock price increases in case of call. The ATM options premium decay curve is as below in figure 10.1; please note that the premium erodes very rapidly within 30 days of the expiry of an option:

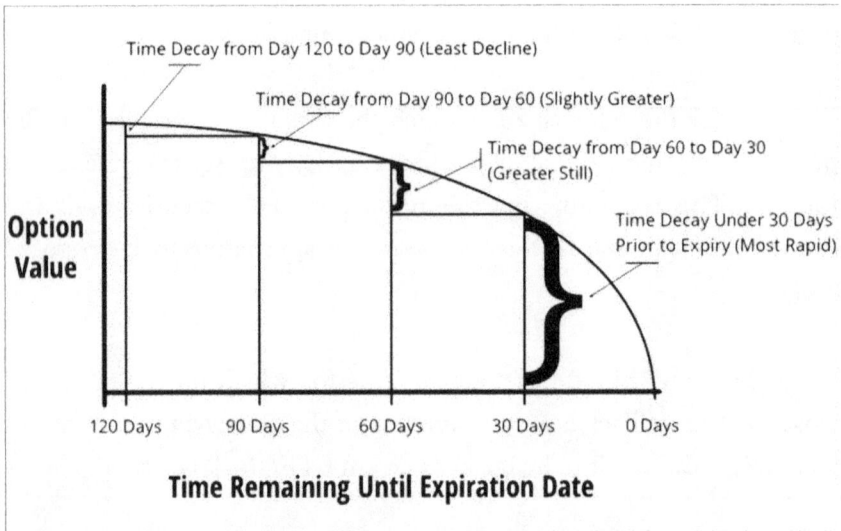

Figure 10.1 ATM options premium decay curve

Let's take the example 9.1: instead of buying the vertical debit call spread if we purchased the calls of strike price 78 only, we should have been subjected to substantial time decay (Theta = -0.746). As we purchased vertical debit call spreads, the time decay has been dampened (by the opposite sold options) to -0.25 only.

In the same token in example 9.2, instead of buying the vertical debit put spread if we purchased the puts of strike price 376 only we should have been subjected to substantial time decay (Theta = -0.712). As we purchased vertical debit put spreads, the time decay has been dampened (by the opposite sold options) to -0.20 only.

The volatility and time decay risks are significantly minimized in At-The-Money vertical spreads. We need to pick the direction (bullish or bearish) of the ETF/stock in this case and so At-The-Money vertical spreads are subjected to directional risk only, otherwise known as Delta.

Most important advantage in ATM debit spread: the best risk to reward ratio and win rate combination

Figure 10.2 below shows the natural relationship between the risk to reward ratio and win rate for different options strategies:

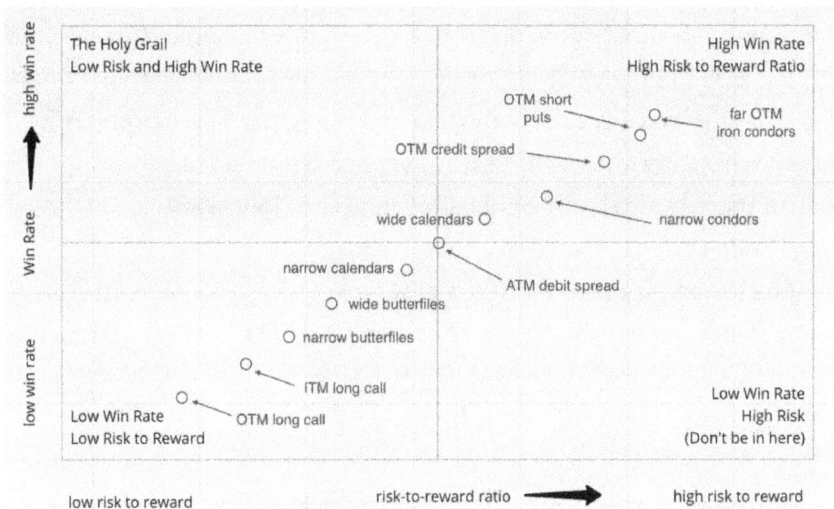

Figure 10.2: Natural relationship between risk to reward ratio and win rate for different options strategies

Courtesy: optionstradiniq.com

Please note that, knowing the win rate of a strategy is not sufficient to determine if one strategy is better than the other; you need to also know the risk to reward ratio for that particular strategy. For example, a strategy that wins 85% of the time is a losing proposition if the average win is $1 and the average loss is $10. In the grid of figure 10.2 above, the upper right corner contains this kind of strategies. The real life example is Iron Condors, they are high probability trade i.e. the win rate is high however the risk-to-reward ratio is also very high. If you've traded iron condors, you've realized that while they win much more often than they lose, one hapless loss may completely wipe out the consolidated capital of multiple wins earlier.

The upper left quadrant of the grid should contain strategies with very high win rate and very low risk-to-reward and is naturally empty as Holy Grail strategies do **not** exist.

The lower right quadrant of the grid should contain strategies with high risk-to-reward and also very low win rate; these are losing strategies and you don't want be in this quadrant of doom. However, no strategies fall in the extreme lower right corner of this quadrant, where the risk-to-reward is extremely high and the win rate is extremely low. Because if such strategies did exist, then a trader could take the opposite side of those trades and would have found the Holy Grail.

The lower left quadrant of the grid represents strategies which have low risk-to-reward also low rate of winning. The real life example is Butterflies, they are low probability trade i.e. the win rate is low however the reward-to-risk ratio is high.

Most interestingly, ATM debit spread is at the center of the quadrants and so has the **best** risk-to-reward and win rate combination. It has neither the low rate of winning like Butterflies not the low reward-to-risk ratio like Iron Condors. If our average loss is equal to about our average win (reward-to-risk ratio = 1), we need to win at least 50% of the time to be profitable. At-The-Money debit spreads have this characteristic. When constructed such that the maximum potential profit is equal to about the debit premium, we need to determine the direction (Delta) correctly in more than 50% of the time to be profitable. The divergence methods in this book determine the direction correctly more than 50% of the time.

This page is intentionally left blank

Eleven

Two Advanced Strategies: Butterfly and Calendar Spread, better than ATM Debit Spread?

> *"What do you need to make a small fortune on Wall Street? - A large fortune."* - Anonymous

Let's revisit the natural relationship diagram between the risk-to-reward ratio and win-rate for several options strategies as described in Figure 10.2 below:

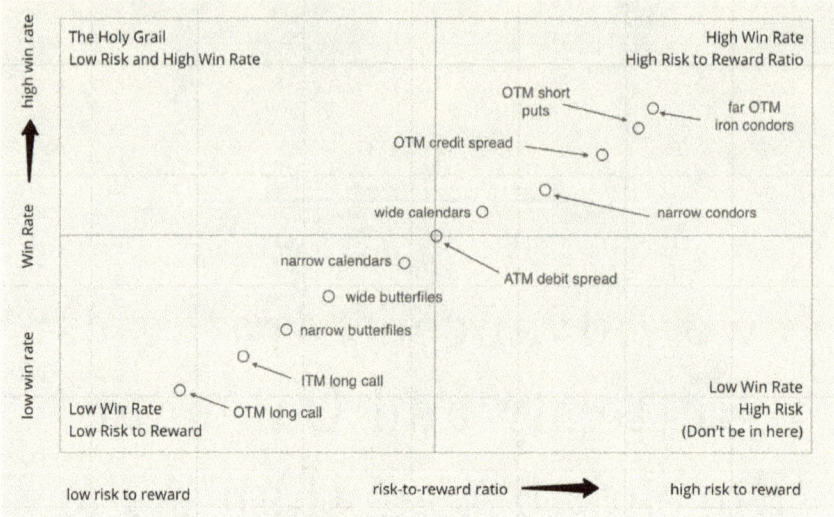

Figure 11.1: Natural relationship between risk to reward ratio and win rate for different options strategies
Courtesy: OptionstradingIQ.com

The strategies under the upper right quadrant are not favorable to the swing traders like us as they do NOT have favorable reward to risk ratios.

However, out of several strategies listed under the lower left quadrant, we have chosen ATM debit spread as our favorite strategy. We have also discussed earlier why should we exclude long Call or long Put. Still, there are two more strategies left that need our attention viz. Butterflies and narrow calendar spreads.

In the lower left quadrant the reward to risk ratio is high but the win rate is low. However, as the divergence between the price action and Stochastic Oscillator is a powerful leading indicator which correctly predicts the upcoming market direction most of the time, by applying this method we can actually improve the win-rate substantially as we were directionally correct and guessed it beforehand.

We will discuss the **debit** Butterfly and **debit** calendar spread only as for the credit Butterfly and calendar spread the reward to risk ratio is very low:

11.1 Butterfly Spread

Butterfly spread is a complex and advanced options strategy, in which two following debit Butterfly spreads will be of our interest: Long Call Butterfly spread and Long Put Butterfly spread.

11.1.1 Long (Debit) Call Butterfly spread

This spread is created by selling two (2) ATM/NTM call options, buying one OTM call option at the higher strike price and buying another ITM call option at the lower strike price. All of these call options must have the same expiration date. You can think long call butterfly spread as a union of two separate call spreads (one debit or bull call spread and one credit or bear call spread) conjoined at the ATM/NTM strike price. Net debit is created when we enter the trade.

Thus, the maximum loss = Net debit paid on premium (excluding commissions),

The maximum profit = ATM/NTM strike of the written option - the strike of the lower call - premium paid (excluding commissions),

Breakeven point(s): There are two breakeven points in Butterfly spread i.e.

The lower breakeven point = lowest strike price + the net debit of the position (excluding commissions) and

The upper breakeven point = highest strike price - the net debit of the position (excluding commissions).

Example and Profit & Loss diagram of long Call Butterfly spread

Let's take the example of our eternal stock ABC (Amerisource-Bergen Corporation) trading at $100.08 and all these calls below will expire after 90 days from now. The Long Call Butterfly with $5 spread and the Profit and Loss diagram are described as below:

Buy 1 ABC 95 call at 6.40	(6.40)
Sell 2 ABC 100 calls at 3.30 (NTM/ATM)	6.60
Buy 1 ABC 105 call at 1.45	(1.45)
Net Debit (i.e. maximum loss) =	(1.25)

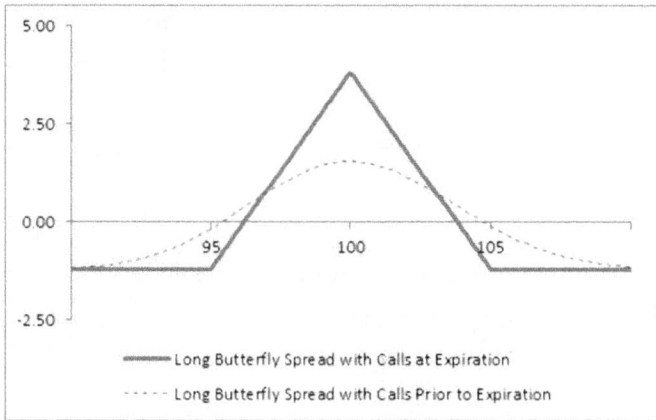

Figure: 11.2 Profit & Loss diagram of Long Call Butterfly for stock ABC
(AmerisourceBergen Corp.)

The maximum profit for the above Butterfly spread = ATM/NTM strike of the written option - the strike of the lower call - premium paid = $100-$95-$1.25= $3.75.

The lower breakeven point = lowest strike price + the net debit of the position = $95+$1.25 = $96.25 and

The upper breakeven point = highest strike price - the net debit of the position = $105-$1.25 = $103.75.

11.1.2 Long (Debit) Put Butterfly spread

This spread is created by selling two (2) ATM/NTM put options, buying one OTM put option at the lower strike price and buying another ITM put option at the higher strike price. All of these put options must have the same expiration date. You can think long put butterfly spread as a union of two separate put spreads (one debit or bear put spread and one credit or bull put spread) conjoined at the ATM/NTM strike price. Net debit is created when we enter the trade.

Thus, the maximum loss = Net debit paid on premium (excluding commissions),

The maximum profit = The strike of the highest put - ATM/NTM strike of the written option - premium paid (excluding commissions),

Breakeven point(s): There are two breakeven points in Butterfly spread i.e.

The lower breakeven point = lowest strike price + the net debit of the position (excluding commissions) and

The upper breakeven point = highest strike price - the net debit of the position (excluding commissions).

Example and Profit & Loss diagram of long Put Butterfly spread

Let's take the example of our eternal stock ABC (Amerisource-Bergen Corporation) trading at $100.08 and all these puts below will expire after 90 days from now. The Long Put Butterfly with $5 spread and the Profit and Loss diagram are described as below:

Buy 1 ABC 105 put at 6.25	(6.25)
Sell 2 ABC 100 puts at 3.15	6.30
Buy 1 ABC 95 put at 1.25	(1.25)
Net debit (i.e. maximum loss) =	(1.20)

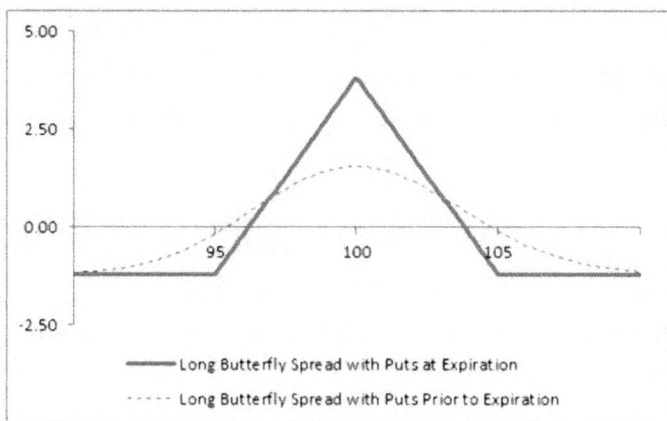

Figure: 11.3 Profit & Loss diagram of Long Put Butterfly for stock ABC
(AmerisourceBergen Corp.)

The maximum profit for the above Butterfly spread = The strike of the highest put - ATM/NTM strike of the written option - premium paid = \$105-\$100-\$1.20=\$3.80.

The lower breakeven point = lowest strike price + the net debit of the position = \$95+\$1.20 = \$96.20 and

The upper breakeven point = highest strike price - the net debit of the position = \$105-\$1.20 = \$103.80.

Strategy discussion on long Call Butterfly

From the Profit and Loss diagram 11.2 it is evident that, a long call butterfly realizes its maximum profit if the stock price equals the center strike price on the expiration date.

The stock price was at or near the center strike price when the position was established; so for long call butterfly the forecast must be "neutral" price action at expiration. As a matter of fact, the long call butterfly is touted as a "neutral" strategy, when the market outlook was "range" bound.

However, if the ETF/stock price was below the center strike price when the position was established, then the forecast for long call butterfly should be "modestly bullish" as for the ETF/stock price to rise to the center strike price at expiration.

As the divergence between the price action and Stochastic Oscillator dictates where the price may eventually go, for bullish divergence, we will apply this "modestly bullish" strategy of long call butterfly. Let me explain this by recalling our earlier example 9.1 below:

On August 22 2023 XBI closed at $78.37 and based on bullish divergence our price target became $80.07. The stop loss was $75.91.

So, instead of creating the Butterfly at the ATM/NTM price of $78, we should create the modestly bullish Butterfly at the target price of $80. The Butterfly was with $2 spread and it's profit and loss diagram was as below:

Buy 10 XBI 78 calls expiry: Nov 23, 2023 at 3.05	(3,050)
Sell 20 XBI 80 calls expiry: Nov 23, 2023 at 2.35	4,700
Buy 10 XBI 82 calls expiry: Nov 23, 2023 at 1.95	(1,950)
Net Debit (or maximum loss) =	(300)

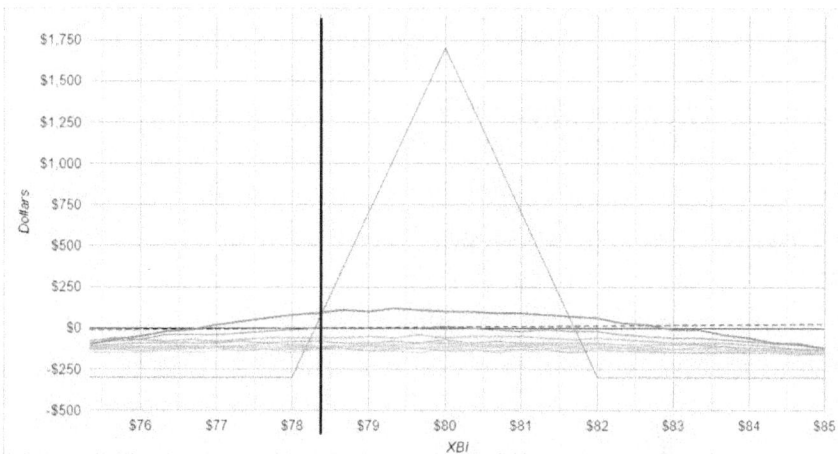

Figure 11.4: Profit and Loss diagram for modestly bullish Butterfly spread of XBI ETF

Please note that, XBI ETF price was at $78.37 (black solid line) August 22, 2023 which was below the center strike price ($80) when the position was established. Stochastic divergence forecast was "modestly bullish" and so we were expecting the ETF price to rise to the center strike price at expiration to maximize our profit.

As expected from the Figure 11.1, the reward-to-risk ratio was also very high for this bullish Butterfly spread:

reward-to-risk =(2,000-300)/300=5.66.

Strategy discussion on long Put Butterfly

From the Profit and Loss diagram 11.3 it is evident that, a long put butterfly realizes its maximum profit if the stock price equals the center strike price on the expiration date.

The stock price was at or near the center strike price when the position was established; so for long put butterfly the forecast must be "neutral" price action at expiration and the market outlook was "range" bound.

If you compare the profit and loss diagrams of 11.2 and 11.3, the long call butterfly and long put butterfly look basically the same. You can create these "neutral" butterflies using either **all** calls or **all** puts or even with one call spread and one put spread. The Butterfly with one call spread and one put spread is called the "iron"-butterfly. The distinct feature of long iron butterfly is that it's a "credit" spread unlike these two debit butterflies.

However, if the ETF/stock price was above the center strike price when the position was established, then the forecast for long put butterfly should be "modestly bearish" as for the ETF/stock price to fall to the center strike price at expiration.

As the divergence between the price action and Stochastic Oscillator dictates where the price may eventually go, for bearish divergence, we will apply this "modestly bearish" strategy of long put butterfly. Let me explain this by recalling our earlier example 9.2 below:

On July 24, 2023 QQQ closed at $376.22 and based on bearish divergence our price target became $372.74. The stop loss became $387.98.

So, instead of creating the Butterfly at the ATM/NTM price of $376, we should create the modestly bearish Butterfly at the target price of $373, which is nearest to $372.74. The Butterfly was with $2 spread and it's profit and loss diagram was as below:

Buy 10 QQQ 371 Puts expiry: Oct 20, 2023 at 11.19	(11,190)
Sell 20 QQQ 373 Puts expiry: Oct 20, 2023 at 11.81	23,620
Buy 10 QQQ 375 Puts expiry: Oct 20, 2023 at 12.64	(12,640)
Net Debit (or maximum loss) =	(210)

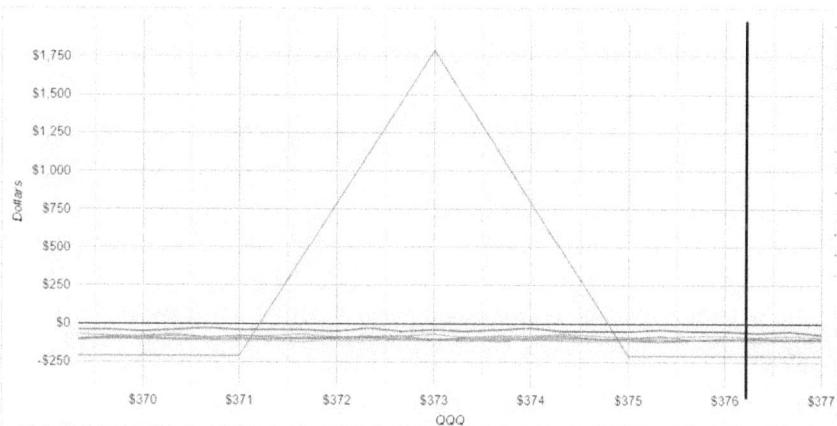

Figure 11.5: Profit and Loss diagram for modestly bearish Butterfly spread of QQQ ETF

Please note that, QQQ ETF price was at $376.22 (black solid line) July 24, 2023 which was above the center strike price ($373) when the position was established. Stochastic divergence forecast was "modestly bearish" and so we were expecting the ETF price to fall to the center strike price at expiration to maximize our profit.

The reward-to-risk ratio was also very high for this bearish Butterfly spread: reward-to-risk =(2,000-210)/210=8.5

Caveats of Butterfly strategy

1. The biggest caveat for the butterfly strategy is that, Butterfly trades are generally very slow moving early on in the trade and that's why Butterfly trades are aptly called the "vacation trade". However, there is no guarantee that the target price will reach at the end of life of the butterfly spread.

If you recall example 9.1 on XBI ETF, the target price was reached after 5 days we placed the trade and for example 9.2 on QQQ ETF, the target price was reached after 7 days we'd placed the trade. And for your information, in both cases, the butterfly spreads **lost** money as the targets were reached "too soon".

2. Butterfly spreads are complex spreads comprising two separate spreads: one debit spread and one credit spread. If things go wrong, adjustment of the butterfly spread could be a problem. The butterfly spreads adjustment is a subject by itself and may occupy a whole fat chapter.

Conclusion on Butterfly spread

Although, butterfly spreads offer better reward-to-risk compared to vertical spread, based on the caveats discussed above, the later seems to be a better strategy for swing trading in terms of simplicity and adjustments.

Butterfly spreads have their own space and could be used in weekly or daily options [From our list of ETFs, as of writing, SPY and QQQ options are expiring daily and IWM options are expiring on Monday, Wednesday and Friday].

Now, let me discuss the second strategy i.e. the (narrow) calendar spread below. First, I will introduce you to the calendar spread and then to the "narrowness" of it.

11.2 Calendar /Narrow Calendar spread

Conceptually, calendar spread is very simple. For vertical call/put spread, we select two different calls/puts with different strike prices however of the same expiration date; but in calendar spread, we select single call/put expiring in two different dates. So, in this case later, the same call or put is temporally distributed and hence the name "calendar".

As we mentioned above, we will only discuss the **debit** calendar spreads as for the credit calendar spreads the reward to risk ratio is very low.

Calendar spreads with a week (or less than a week for daily options) in expiration span are generally considered as "narrow" calendar spreads and the calendars with larger expiration span (including monthly) are considered as "wide" calendar spreads.

Wide calendar spread example

During the opening session on February 3, 2022, we'd decided to trade a debit put calendar spread on stock Travelers Company (TRV).

As it does not have options with weekly expirations, we used the next available monthly expiration as below:

Closing Price of TRV = $173.28. We wrote the NTM/ATM calendar spread at $175 strike price.

Sell 10 Feb 22 TRV $175 put @ $4.05, Buy 10 March 18 TRV $175 put @ $6.50.

The total debit (i.e. the maximum probable loss) became $2,450 (excluding commission). The Profit and Loss diagram for this calendar spread was as below:

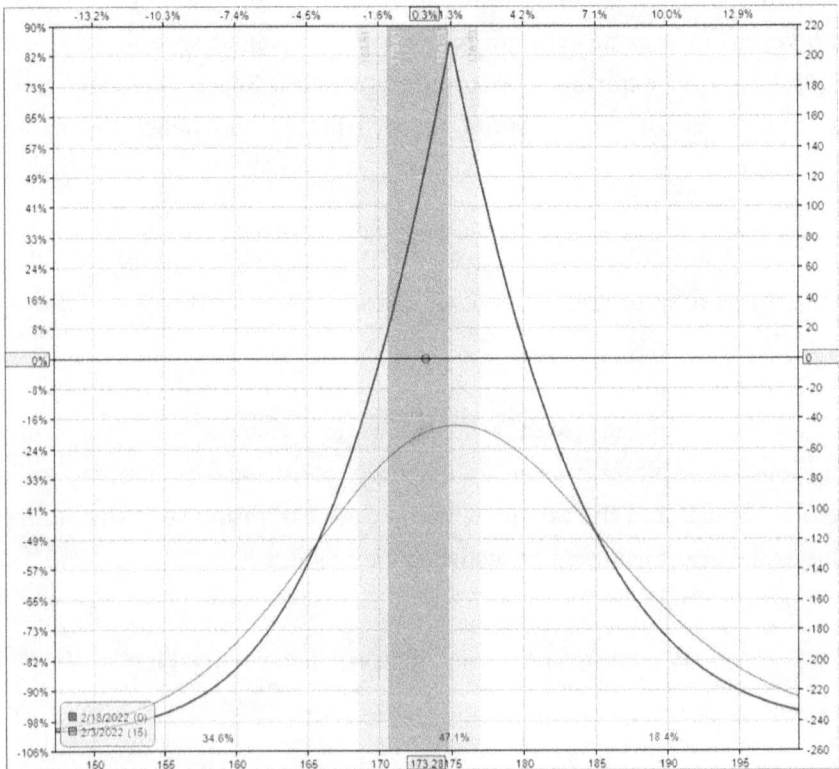

Figure 11.6: Profit and Loss Diagram for Monthly Debit Put Calendar Spread for Stock TRV

In Calendar Spread, we can never have the exact maximum profit number (can you tell, why?) and from the option-tool provided by my broker, the maximum profit was calculated and which was about $2,100 for this trade (see the tip of the tent of figure 11.6 above).

So, the reward-to-risk ratio = $2,100/$2,450 = 0.86. This is a terrible reward-to-risk ratio which also conforms Figure 11.1 (that the reward-to-risk ratio of wide calendar spread is low). Now let us see how the reward-to-risk ratio improves in "narrow" calendar spread.

Narrow Calendar spread example

Here is an SPY calendar that is only five (5) days apart in expirations. During the opening session on February 3, 2022, we'd decided to trade a debit put calendar spread on SPY ETF.

Closing Price of SPY = $453.60. We wrote the NTM/ATM calendar spread at $454 strike price.

Sell 10 Feb 25 SPY 454 put @ $8.55; Buy 10 Mar 2 SPY 454 put @ $9.35.

The total debit (i.e. the maximum probable loss) became $800 (excluding commission). The Profit and Loss diagram for this calendar spread was as below:

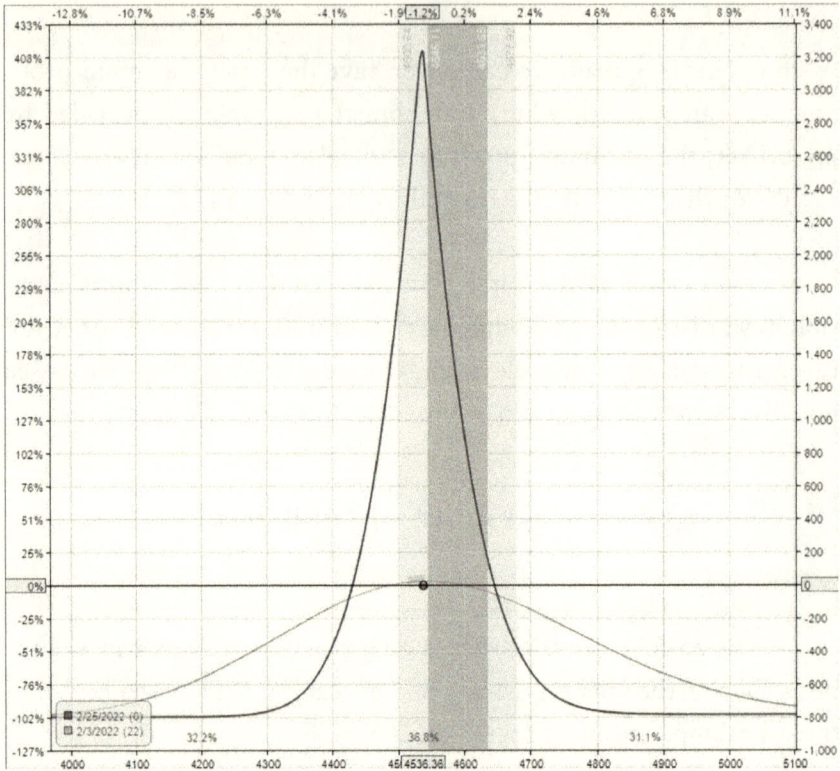

Figure 11.7: Profit and Loss Diagram for "narrow" (Less than Weekly expiration) Debit Put Calendar Spread for SPY

Again, from the option-tool provided by my broker, the maximum profit was calculated and which was about $3,200 for this calendar spread and the reward-to-risk ratio=$3,200/$8,00=4 which is an impressive ratio.

It's evident from the graphs of debit butterfly and calendar spread that, structure wise these two type of trades are extremely similar. Both creates a "tent" like structure with the highest profit potential at the tip and maximum loss incurs at the "wing" like structures of the butterfly and calendar spread.

As explained in the strategy discussions of butterfly spreads above, when the bullish or bearish divergences between the price and stochastic appears, we will **not** create "neutral" narrow calendar spreads but will create modestly bullish or bearish "narrow" calendar spreads based on the target prices.

Now you probably also guessed that, there is no guarantee that the target price will reach during the very narrow life (week or less) of the narrow calendar spread. This is the biggest disadvantage of using narrow calendar spread in swing trading using divergence (between the price action and stochastic oscillator).

Conclusion on narrow Calendar spread

Although, narrow calendar spread (expiring in a week or less) offers better reward-to-risk compared to vertical spread, based on the discussion above, it is evident that the later is a better strategy for swing trading.

Narrow calendar spreads have their own space and could be used successfully with weekly or daily expirations however not in our case of swing trading which requires far more temporally extended structures.

This page is intentionally left blank

Twelve

Money Management

"Risk cannot be eliminated; it just gets transferred and spread."
– Howard Marks

Money Management is a pivotal part of a trading system. It can make or break any system, however good it is. If proper money management technique is not employed, the market can put an end to your account with a single hapless loss and get you out of the business. In this chapter I'm going to discuss some salient points on money management as below:

Diversification

For a system to have the highest odds of profitability over time and markets the inescapable tradeoff is volatility; this is another universal market behavior. Diversification can be used, of course, but it can only dampen the volatility so much.

Warren Buffett famously stated that "Diversification is protection against ignorance. It makes little sense if you know what you are

155

doing." In Buffett's view, studying a couple of financial instruments in great depth and using that knowledge to profit on those instruments is more lucrative than spreading a portfolio across a broad array of financial instruments so that gains from certain instruments offset losses from others and produce mediocre results at best.

Influenced by Oracle of Omaha's recommendation, I'm also not a big fan of diversifying too much by trading with a big sundry list of ETFs.

Probably the single most important and optimal rule in money management is to not expose more than 5% of your capital at risk in a single trade. Please follow this rule by exposing no more than 5% of capital risk in a single instrument.

Don't pay highest (i.e. ask) price while buying options or receive lowest (i.e. bid) price while selling options

Those ETFs as discussed in Chapter V are generally very liquid and so the regular options for them are also very liquid with lots of open interests and volume. This implies that, the spread between the ask and bid price should also be very tight for those ETF options.

In ideal situations, those ETF options which accept $0.01 increment, the spread between the ask and bid price should be $0.02. (**Important Note:** Under Penny Pilot Program, there are some ETF options which accept only $0.05 increment; for them the ideal spread between the ask and bid price should be $0.10).

Following is the real life example of one ideal quote:

SPY August 18, 2023, 442 put premium: Bid: 5.94, Ask: 5.96, Mid: 5.95.

However, in many situations, although the options are very liquid the spreads are **not** kept that tight and uninformed buyers may buy options paying the highest (i.e. ask) price and sell options accepting the lowest (i.e. bid) price.

But, we can definitely bargain with the market makers to get the best price for buying and selling both. Also, as we deal with both buying and selling options in debit spreads, this concept is very important to us.

The rules of thumb to get the best price for buying and selling options are as below:

- For buying options always place the **Buy Limit price** as bid price + $0.02 (in case of options with $0.05 increment place the limit price as bid price + $0.10)
- For selling options always place the **Sell Limit price** as ask price - $0.02 (in case of options with $0.05 increment place the limit price as ask price - $0.10)
- Wait for 10 minutes. You will see either the price has been accepted or some price adjustments have been made (by the market maker). If the price has not been accepted repeat the same steps above and wait for another 10 minutes. More often than not, your price will be accepted within 30 minutes of this exercise.

Example: TLT August 18, 2023, 102 put premium: Bid: 1.51, Ask: 1.65. (Note: the spread is more than $0.02)

For buying this put option, we will place the Buy Limit price as $1.53. By this, we are asking the market maker to tighten the spread to

$0.02. And we will repeat the process in 10 minutes interval (with the new bid price) until the limit order has been accepted.

For selling this put option we will place the Sell Limit price as $1.63. By this, we are asking the market maker to tighten the spread to $0.02. And we will repeat the process in 10 minutes interval (with the new ask price) until the limit order has been accepted.

Based on my practical experiences (and also of many fellow traders) on this it seems that, market makers don't like these type of orders and get annoyed and they accept them most of the time going out of the way, to maintain the order flow of the market as they desire after our orders.

Subscribe to one inexpensive Stock Price Alert Service which will give you a call

In our trading methodology described in Chapter 9 and 10, as soon the target price is reached or stop-loss is hit, we need to exit the trade immediately. As we cannot and will not monitor the ETF like day traders, I strongly recommend to subscribe to an inexpensive stock alert service which will call your phone in the event of the target price is reached or the stop-loss is hit.

I'm subscribed to **StockAlarm** application, which is truly inexpensive ($9.99/month for unlimited alerts) and does a great job as soon as my stock hits the target price or the stop-loss. Please note that, I am not affiliated with this company.

Minimization of frictional costs

The last part of money management is the minimization of frictional costs. The trading industry drains substantial amount of money from the traders in the form of exchange fees, regulatory fees, data fees, brokerage fees etc. and these fees are the frictional costs of trading. We must pay these fees irrespective of the outcome of the trades we take.

Out of this array of fees, we can *only* control the brokerage fee. To achieve the lowest possible transaction costs, look for the brokers with the lowest possible commission. Don't be shy bargaining for even lower rates and watch intensely and regularly as they are notorious for escalating rates and keeping you uninformed. If practicable, keep changing brokers after two years or so.

Formula on calculating total no. of contracts based on risk taken:

This paragraph includes the calculation for total number of contracts we can trade based on our risk capital as below:

If 'C' is the principal amount and 'G' is the risk taken in percent (0<G<=5 in our case), the Risk Capital (R) is defined as R=C*G*0.01.

If 'P' is the premium paid for one (1) ETF/Stock vertical ATM/NTM debit spread, the total no. of contracts we can trade can be defined as N=floor(R/(P*100)) where floor () is a function which returns the **lower** integer by rounding a decimal number.

Example:

C (Principal amount) =$20,000, G (risk taken in percent) =5, P (premium paid for a single ETF/Stock for the ATM/NTM vertical debit spread) =3.75

Risk Capital (R) =20000*5*0.01=$1000

Total number of contracts we can trade (N) = floor (1000/375) = 2 (floor of 2.66)

Index

S

screener
  59
SEC
  21, 59, 61
sector
  51–54, 57
securities
  7, 21, 23, 27, 38, 46–48, 55, 61, 66, 78, 83, 85
  98–99, 102, 107–8, 130–31
  treasury
    38, 52, 55
shorting
  5–8, 16, 19, 27, 39–40, 46–48, 58–59, 61, 76, 78–79, 82, 95–96
  100, 117, 129–31
  synthetically
    39
SMA
  102–3
spreads
  38, 44, 49, 59–60, 76, 83, 105–11, 117–27, 129–35, 137–53, 155–60
SQQQ
  40–42, 44
stochastics
  12, 93, 97–100, 111–14, 116, 122, 138, 144–47, 153
stocks
  5, 8, 20–24, 28, 33–39, 46–48, 59, 61, 63, 66, 70–72, 79–80
  82–83, 86–92, 97, 106–9, 114–15, 117–18, 123, 129–33, 140–44, 146, 149–50,
158–61
  stop
    39, 46–48, 96–97, 114–15, 120, 123–25, 144, 146, 158
  trail
    96

T

tail
  13
tax

Sudipta (pronounced "sue-deep-toe") Datta, an Information Technology (IT) consultant, brings extensive professional expertise to the realm of Financial Institutions. In addition, he maintains personal interest in ETFs, stocks, options and futures markets. With a market tenure spanning sixteen years, Sudipta is a seasoned veteran as well as an accomplished private investor.

Sudipta holds BS and MS degrees in IT and Computer Engineering. He lives in the suburb of Houston, Texas with his wife, two young-adult sons and two Fido boys.